Paul Hostovsky

MORE SELECTED POEMS

FUTURECYCLE PRESS

www.futurecycle.org

Cover photo by ClickerHappy (Rudy and Peter Skitterians); cover and interior design by Diane Kistner; Gentium Book Basic text and Cronos Pro titling

Library of Congress Control Number: 2025950892

Published by FutureCycle Press
Athens, Georgia, USA

ISBN 978-1-952593-53-6

Contents

Foreword

from
THE BAD GUYS

from
IS THAT WHAT THAT IS

Foreword

Paul Hostovsky is our heartfelt story-teller poet, our risible raconteur of daily life, a poet in love with memory who keeps finding new ways of taking us by the hand and leading us back, putting us under the spell of his own personal Mnemosyne. You owe it to yourself to hear his voice.

I first became aware of Hostovsky's work a dozen years ago, when I wrote an essay for Poetry Corner on several poems from his earlier collections, books that are represented in his 2014 *Selected Poems* volume. Time has moved on, of course, as has Hostovsky, and it is time for a *More Selected Poems* volume from FutureCycle Press, this time with poems drawn from *The Bad Guys* (2015), *Is That What That Is* (2017), *Late for the Gratitude Meeting* (2019), *Mostly* (2021), *Pitching for the Apostates* (2023), and *Perfect Disappearances* (2025).

Since I have read virtually all of Hostovsky's published poetry, you might well ask me if I have a favorite poem of his—and I do. It is called "Going Back," and if you are standing in a bookstore reading this foreword and wondering whether to buy this book, I would urge you not to take my word for it but turn to page 79 and read it for yourself. It's a fantasy poem, in which Hostovsky is allowed to go back in time and chat with the "lonely, bored, back-row kid" he was when he was growing up:

> ...I picture us sitting
> on a bench in Taylor Park, one of his PF Fliers
> jackhammering nervously next to my sensible shoes...

Grown-up Paul answers as many of growing-up Paul's questions as he can, and then asks him, "Is there anything else you'd like to know?"

> He takes a minute to think. Then asks, "Are you happy?"
> Oh yes, in fact (and I start to choke up a little) being here now
> with you, I am happier than I have ever been in my life.

I have read "Going Back" dozens of times, and it always has the same effect: when I hit those last three lines, my eyes fill with tears. They just do. And I suspect yours might as well if you read the full poem. That is just Hostovsky being the poetic magician that he is. And he *is* a magician, I am convinced of it. Take these lines from "Perfect Disappearances":

> ...and walk off into the world alone
> with the whole world in your hand. God
> help the writers in love with the words that disappear
> like disappearing trains you catch
> by running after them,
> losing a shoe, a hat, an earring, a spouse—a lifetime
> of chasing the disappearing words,
> breathlessly reaching for them,

grabbing hold and hoisting yourself up
onto the caboose, entering the rhythm
of those corridors moving through the world...

In spite of all the magic, Hostovsky sometimes likes to portray himself as congenitally disagreeable, a regular Grumpy of Seven Dwarfs fame, as in his poem "Grr":

I love the grouchy words—
peevish, irascible, fractious—
I am all of them—crabby, morose,
snarky and more. I hate the phrase
"and more." It's so American, so
manifest destiny...
....Listen,
don't be an asshole if you can help it.
But if you can't help it, help
others to understand the assholes.
Be an ambassador of assholes....

But somehow I'm not buying it, at least not all of it. Because on the flipside there's the love—there's always the love—buried inside every Hostovsky poem. As in these closing lines of "Commandment":

...You gotta love
your neighbor as yourself,
but if your neighbor is
irritating, try loving
all your irritations, try
getting in touch with
the oneness of their long
branching history, whose
latest leafy unclenching
florid blossom you are.
It's a numinous workaround
and you gotta love it.

There is so much more to Hostovsky and his poetry that I don't have the space to describe here: his ambiguous attitude toward his Jewish heritage ("I boycotted / my own bar mitzvah"), his flustered youthful response when his first girlfriend invited him to unbutton her blouse ("It felt like unwrapping a present that I'd only seen advertised / in magazines"), his marital adventures ("I married my sign language teacher / who was Deaf, and it didn't work out, so I married another / Deaf woman, which didn't work out either, so I married a third / Deaf woman and the third time's the charm"), his absolutely passionate love for his main gig as an American Sign Language interpreter ("The active listening of Deaf people / in their signed conversations / with each other, if you've ever / seen them—beautiful, flitting, / leaping—communication as communion"), or his realization that, at his stage in life, observing can be more enjoyable than participating ("I would rather / read a poem about bicycles than ride a bicycle").

It seems only fitting to close with Hostovsky's reminder to us all about the unique role poetry can play in our lives, a lesson he says he ultimately learned from the nameless, faceless pilferer who stole a book of his poems:

To the One Who Stole a Book at My Poetry Reading

Good writers borrow, great writers steal,
they say. I say it belonged to you already—
the sounds of the words, the spell of the words,
and the words themselves, they belong
to all of us. As do the silences. As does
the breath. Ours the air in the room, ours
the shared mouth where the words live,
ours the deepest listening. Listen, after
the reading, when they lined up to buy my book,
it felt a little like extortion: me taking their money
and giving them back what was already theirs.
Poetry belongs to everyone. And to no one.
Kudos to you for insisting on that. Thank you
for reminding me my poems aren't my poems.

—Carl M. Jenks, *Poetry Corner,* January 2026

from
THE BAD GUYS

(FutureCycle Press, 2015)

In the Home for Elderly Vehicular Manslaughterers by the Sea

The guilt, like the sand, is in everything,
being so near, as they are, to the ocean,
being so close, as they were, to the end
of their lives, before they took the lives
they took. Someone should have taken
the keys away. In many cases, they tried—
but the old, mottled, gnarled knuckles
clenched, closing reflexively around
that silver promise, its heft, its glinting
mountainous teeth. And they held on to it.
Now the guilt, like the sand, is on their hands
and on their lips. It's the grit in the food
they can't eat. Lucky the demented ones,
with no idea, no memory, blithely chewing.

To the Lady Who Gave Out Pencils on Halloween

I would like to say thank you,
because I don't think I said thank you
once in all those years
that I climbed your steep front steps
in my mask or sheet or wig or witch's hat
and held up my opened pillow case
among the other opened pillow cases
like so many straining baby-bird mouths
in the hope that you would finally come around
to our sweet-tooth point of view. Which you never did.
So we mocked you, and we spurned you,
and we littered your lawn with our candy wrappers,
our chewed gum the sweet had gone out of,
the rinds and sticks of the much-lauded,
much-coveted candied apples your neighbor
Mrs. Schachtel gave out each year—the syrupy
antithesis to your dry and austere
number two pencils. But they survived,
it needs to be said; when all that sugary
frivolity melted away, your stiffly formal
wooden gifts remained, like so many horizontal
soldiers standing at attention at the bottom
of the bag. Deployed in kitchen drawers,
desk drawers, jars jammed with pens, pencils,
brushes, penknives, magic markers, emery boards,
they were mostly overlooked, forgotten. Some of them
probably outlived my entire childhood. A few
probably outlived you. It's entirely possible
that one or two—this one, for example,
which feels as sharp as the day it was first
sharpened—could outlive me, too.

Slapstick

The three stooges weren't funny anymore
after Kenny Hovanek stopped me in the park
and slapped me in the face and knocked
my books down. Suddenly Moe looked
a lot like Hitler without the mustache.
And Larry and Curly looked like
what I must have looked like to Kenny Hovanek
who chuckled sadistically, shook his head, swaggered
away. My cheek stung for days. My father
went on chuckling right there beside me
on the paisley couch in front of our television,
but our favorite show had changed forever
and I couldn't tell him why. If I laughed now
it was a forced laugh, so he wouldn't know
I'd met force in the park, met it with nothing
but tears. Which hurt more than the blow.
It was torture, sitting there next to him,
laughing at the pain, laughing through the pain,
but I never cracked; I never said a word.

Hitler Stamp

I traded ten triangular
Mongolian stamps for Hitler,
Hitler who killed my father's
whole family.

My father hated Hitler.
He refused to say Hitler's name.
He refused to let anyone say it
under his roof. He refused

to speak a word of German
after 1945. I hated
Hitler, too. But I loved
my Hitler stamp.

I loved taking him out
of the wax-paper sleeve
in my stamp collecting book
and holding him in my hand

under the light. And what
would my father have said if he knew
I was up there in my room
under his roof

hoarding Hitler, harboring Hitler,
holding Hitler up
to the light?

Song

A suicide bomber isn't born a suicide bomber.
He wasn't a suicide bomber in elementary school
when he drew a spiky, yellow, exploding sun

above a little town between two green hills
and gave it to the teacher, and the teacher smiled.
On the day the suicide bomber was born

his father danced through the market from stall
to stall, singing the good news out until
the spiky, yellow, exploding sun went down

over the little town, and by then all the people
in the houses huddled between two green hills
had heard of the birth of the suicide bomber

who wasn't a suicide bomber at all, at all.
He was never in his life what you would call
a suicide bomber. He was his father's son

till that day in the market, the people and animals
splattering like so many fruits and vegetables—
That was the day the suicide bomber was born.
An exploding sun. Like millions of exploding suns.

Bobby Bro

The real names are so much sexier
and the innocent don't need protecting
now that they're in their sixties, clean and sober,
with their mothers dead or demented.
So Bobby Bro was his real name.
He should have been a famous quarterback
with a name like that. Or a movie star,
a prizefighter, a golf pro, a lead singer, a lead
scorer. He was sexy and ragged and he scored
with the hottest girls in my high school
mostly because, without fail, he could score
weed. Which is what he was most famous for.

He wore a silver hemostat on a gold chain
around his neck. It caught the light and winked
as he twisted his torso in the passenger seat
of my mother's car, accepting the diminishing roach
from the hand passing it forward from the backseat.
Then, with the manual dexterity of a surgeon,
he disengaged the hemostat's locking mechanism,
eyed the tip narrowly, clamped the roach
perpendicular to its axis, like a blood vessel
or a fallopian tube awaiting ligation,
raised it up to an almost imperceptible
flaxen mustache and sucked vigorously,

surrendering it to me with popping eyes,
farting lips and inflated cheeks. As for my mother,
she never met Bobby Bro, nor heard his real name uttered,
because I always invented an alias,
a poor substitute, a travesty really, as I made up
my alibis for where I was going and what
I was doing with her car—which I always returned
with all the windows down, after smoking the requisite
ratifying bone to seal the sale with Bobby Bro
and his great and good name.

Dueling Banjos

He was a fingerpicker and I was a frailer,
and she was this beautiful dark-haired guitar
with this forthright mischief in her eyes,
this clef tattooed above her sacrum,
this mother-of-pearl shiver she sent up

my fifteen-year-old spine. I was in love with her,
me, a masturbator in God's eyes as I locked
the door, closed my eyes, and my mouth
sang mute accompaniment to my own frailing
hand: traditional enough, but back then

I thought I'd go blind if I kept it up. Then Doc
Watson came to town with that happy guileless
Tennessee voice, that flatpicking style as clean
as a ringing bell, and his son Merle on banjo.
We both bought tickets and asked her to go.

You know how this story ends. She goes with him,
the fingerpicker. And I can't stop crying.
And I can't stop frailing. And six months later
Merle dies in a tragic tractor accident,
and Doc stops singing for a long, long time.

Rebound Banjo

She left him for her ex
who played the 5-string banjo
in a bluegrass band and whom
she'd left for him—and not
three months before—for a short

sweet-smelling spring,
wound him like a string around
the tuning peg of her index,
touched him and he stiffened,
and he sang. And he broke

down and wept when she went back
to her banjo-playing ex
like a second thought about
a second fiddle, a repeating
chorus or refrain. So he went out west

to forget her. But he couldn't forget—
he saw her everywhere, saw her hands
in the hands of strangers, saw her hair
on the heads of strangers, saw her breasts
in the shapes of the Grand Tetons

high against the big Wyoming sky
at twilight. And on a side street
in Jackson, he saw it in the window
of the pawn shop, its slender neck adorned
with mother-of-pearl inlay,

its fifth tuning peg indented like
a new paragraph, a new chapter,
its pale full-moon face a blank
slate. And he bought it for fifty bucks
which included the case, capo, strap, three

fingerpicks and a Mel Bay's Learn to Play
the Five-String Banjo book. He was
motivated. To win her back, of course.
And of course he didn't win her back.
But he did learn to play in a frailing way

"Cripple Creek" and "Old Joe Clark"
and "Sail Away Ladies Sail Away."

My Underpants

I found them on the bathroom floor
after my cousin and her boyfriend
left for Ithaca. They were green
with gold stripes and they weren't
mine. I stood there for a long time
considering them. They weren't
dirty but they weren't exactly clean
either. They were unwashed.
But they weren't unclean the way
a dead bird is unclean, or the way
an unsanctified thing or an unholy thing
is unclean. I picked them up, and did I
smell them? I want to say I smelled them.
I may have smelled them because
they weren't unclean and they were undoubtedly
my cousin's boyfriend's and he is a good man,
not a holy man but a good man with a good
job in Ithaca, New York and an excellent beard.
Of course I thought about returning them,
sending them back in a mailer or small brown box,
and I thought about washing them,
though they weren't mine and they weren't
unclean, only unwashed, and they weren't
sexy, only colorful. They were more colorful
than all of my underpants put together.
You will want to know I am wearing them
as I write this. Much time has elapsed
since that day in the bathroom. My cousin
and her boyfriend have gotten married.
I have gotten married myself. My wife
has no idea about the provenance
of the green underpants. She thinks they are mine.
She washes them with my underpants
and her underpants, and she puts them all
in a sweet-smelling pile on top of the dresser.
I think there is something a little holy
about a pile of clean underpants on top of a dresser.
I think that putting them away in a drawer
would be like putting your light under a bushel,
or like locking a bird up in a cage,
or like packing up a good green thing
in a small brown box
and sending it far, far away from you.

The Only Question

She was very beautiful.
Exceptionally beautiful.
Beautiful in the way of
certain sudden realizations,
like: My god, is it raining?
or: Look how huge the moon!

She was at the poetry reading.
My poetry reading. Just one among
many pretty undergraduates
until the Q&A. That was when
she raised her hand in the third row
and asked me: "What inspires you?"

What I should have said was:
"Beauty. Beauty inspires me."
And left it at that. And let
the awkward silence speak
for itself while I stared at her
from up at the podium for perhaps

a whole minute, ignoring
the chair of the English Department
clearing his throat, the few diffuse
titters filling the room, the enormous
moon filling the big picture
window as my drenched gaze

fell on her, steadily, like a fine summer
rain falling on the second seat
in the third row. But what I said instead,
a little dryly, was: "Literature. Great
literature inspires me." And she looked
away. And hers was the only question.

Tenth Grade Vocabulary List

I put them all in alphabetical order—
apposite, betwixt, crenellated, duenna,
etcetera—on 8 x 5 index cards,
with their definitions on the back
in etymological order, and studied them
all alone in my room. But in order
to own them, to internalize them,
to be able to retrieve them at the drop
of a word, I knew I needed to use them,
to say them, to embed them in
my sentences. "Please pass the friable,
crenellated chicken pot pie betwixt
the sweet potatoes and green beans,
duenna," I said to my mother
at dinner. She looked over her shoulder
and winced, as though I'd fired a volley
of vocabulary over her head, nicking
her earlobe, embedding itself in the wall
like shrapnel. There's no getting around it,
the big words are intimidating, formidable,
redoubtable, apposite and sometimes
the opposite of apposite. But a hairless,
feckless, rangy kid who didn't know
how to fight, and didn't have a girlfriend,
could use them to good advantage,
to parley, and to parlay, and at parties
to impress girls, blow his rivals away.

Lloyd

I had a friend named Lloyd when I was eight.
I will always remember Lloyd for his two l's
which came at the beginning. I didn't know
much. But I knew two l's could come at the beginning
already at the tender age of eight. Life went
on. I learned about llamas. And Prince Llewellyn.
And the Iliad, which doesn't have two l's
at the beginning, though it kind of looks like it does.
And eventually I lost touch with Lloyd although
I never forgot him. Because every single unlikely
superfluous thing, every odd doubling or identical
twin at the beginning of anything, reminds me of Lloyd
and his two l's: the first one loud, capital, rushing in,
the second one silent, reticent, redundant as Lloyd himself.

Works for Trumpet

We are listening to Alison Balsom
play Bach. "Do we have to

listen to this?" Amber, eleven,
buckled up in the passenger seat,

balks, bucks. We're late for school—
her backpack, lunchbox, and violin

ride mutely in the back. She looks
down at the CD box, makes a face:

"Who is *Botch,* anyway?"
Her violin leaps violently to the floor

as I brake for a stopped school bus.
"It's not *Botch,*" I tell her. "It's *Bach*—

only the greatest musician who ever lived,
that's who." She gives the box a second,

closer look—"Bach is pretty. How old is Bach?"—
frowning at the photo of Alison Balsom

on the cover. "That's not Bach," I tell her.
"It's Alison Balsom. On trumpet. And yes,

she *is* pretty." Amber raises her left eyebrow,
then stitches it to its twin. "A *girl*

playing the trumpet?" And I can hear
the wheels turning, tuning, inside her head

as the school bus trundles dumbly along
and I follow close behind. "There aren't

any girls who play trumpet in *my* school.
Only boys." And Alison belts out another

string of impossibly gorgeous arpeggios.
And Amber looks out the window, scratches

her head. She is listening. I don't say
a word, pull in behind the school bus, park,

and we sit there for a long time, the violin
on the floor, the trumpet in the air, Alison

Balsom breathing Bach, breathing beauty,
Amber late for school and listening hard.

Spiritual Mom

Mom got spiritual in her late fifties,
and we really had no patience for all
the forgiveness. It was disconcerting
the way she'd kneel down on the floor
in the middle of the conversation
and hug the dog, whispering affirmations
into its long ear, stroking and folding it
inside out like a pocket. When she emptied
her bank account and gave all the money
to whoever asked, wandering around downtown,
reaching into her purse to offer whatever
her fingers touched first, it was the last
straw. We did an intervention, as they call it
in the field of addiction. We sat her down
and confronted her on her spiritual habit.
The room grew quiet as Mom wept softly,
her eyes searching the floor for what to say.
The silence was terrible—even the dog
cocked its head in that doglike listening way
for some kind of affirmation that Mom
had heard us, and understood, and would cease
her spiritual ways, or at least be in the world
a little more and no longer walking around like
she didn't have a colon, with one foot in Heaven
and an ear to the hot little mouth of God.

The Meteorologist's Breasts

which are right next to the hurricane
which is inching up the East Coast
are lovely and on the small side.
The hurricane is predicted to be
the biggest to hit the East Coast
since they started naming hurricanes
in 1953. *Love is greater than fear*
said the bumper sticker on the truck
in front of me in traffic. It took
three and a half hours to get home.
Her blouse is soft and blue and stretchy.
When I lose power she goes on pointing
to Atlantic City, smiling bravely.

Gauguin's Grandson

was named Paul Gauguin,
too. He was an artist,
too. He lived in Denmark
in his grandfather's shadow
all his life. And he chafed
against that shadow.
Like living under a rock—
a rock as big as the biggest
island in French Polynesia.
He painted only insects.
Insects that live under rocks—
beetles, ants, centipedes,
pill bugs. In a later period,
he painted only his wife Marta
in only her long black hair
and horn-rimmed glasses.
Toward the end of his life
he made hundreds of collages
of orthopterous insects—
katydids, mantids, cicadas,
crickets and grasshoppers
with long hind legs for jumping
or, you could say, flying;
and for making a rasping, chafing
sound or, you could say, song.

The Emperor's New Clothes

I stole a bathmat
from the Royal Copenhagen Hotel

because it said *Royal Copenhagen* on it
and how cool is that

for stepping out of your shower onto
every day of your life in America

as a souvenir
of a few dissolute days in Denmark?

I like to snuggle the rich velvety pile
with my ten poor stubby toes

while I'm still dripping from the shower,
which is where I get all my best ideas—

then I feel a little like Soren Kierkegaard,
and a little like King Frederick,

and a little like Hans Christian Andersen
getting out of his claw-foot tub

and getting a great idea,
and standing there for a few timeless

dripping moments,
then rushing to his writing table

and spinning the yarn, still naked,
in one inspired sitting,

his trail of wet footprints disappearing
before the ink has dried.

Defense Secretary Slips on Ice

I bet he didn't
see that one coming.
Invisible enemy.
Crushed the phalanx
of his little finger
trying to break his fall
on his own front steps,
rushing out the door this morning
to the big meeting,
a big black-and-blue mark
blooming on his bum now.
The newspapers aren't saying
anything about his bum,
but I bet it hurts like hell to sit
down at the peace table.
He's probably wincing right now.
Which may be why
we're all still at war.
Another beautiful fall
morning, cold and wet,
the air full of the crisp,
exquisite smells of death.

Dooley for State Rep

A small band of supporters
holding up signs and waving
on the corner of Pleasant and Main
on this gelid November morning—and who
is Dooley? He's the one among them
who isn't wearing a hat, the one
with the gelled hair, very red
ears, frozen smile, waving at me
as I drive by, the wind chill
minus twenty, his breath sending out
these little diplomatic envoys
of wispy white warmth every which way.
This man without the hat, without
the sense to put on a hat in weather
like this, this man who wants my vote,
who wants to represent me in the capital,
this man who made the bad decision
to forgo the hat this morning because
it would cover his excellent hair,
or it would make him look weak
when he needs to look strong,
needs to look excellent, and I think
this is exactly what's wrong with America
and its leaders and its image in the eyes
of the world: it all comes down to this
hat, which this man who wants my vote
but shall not have it, doesn't have on.

from
IS THAT WHAT THAT IS

(FutureCycle Press, 2017)

One Ambition

All I ever really wanted
was to whistle with my fingers—

I knew I would never
be the one up on stage

blowing everybody away
with beauty, brilliance, virtuosity...

But to be the lightning
inside the thunderous applause,

to have the audacity
and the manual dexterity

to make a siren screeching
through a dark auditorium,

to be the killer hawk
in all that parroting, pattering rain,

to be, finally, the very best at praise—
now that was something

I thought that if I gave my life to
I might attain.

The Calculus

My hygienist likes to include me
in the decision making.
"Shall we use the hand scaler
or the ultrasonic today?" she asks me.
I like the way she says "we,"
like we're doing something intimate
and collaborative,
like building a snowman,
or more like dismantling one
after an ice storm, flake
by frozen flake. "The calculus
is caused by precipitation
of minerals from your saliva," she explains.
"You can't remove it with your toothbrush.
Only a professional can do that." She's very
professional. She doesn't dumb it down.
"Pay more attention to the lingual side
of your mandibular anteriors," she says.
I love it when she talks like that.
I love the names of teeth: incisor, third molar, bicuspid,
eye-tooth. Her own teeth are
virtuosic. "*Calculus* comes from the Greek
for stone," she says. "In mathematics
it's counting with stones. In medicine,
it's the mineral buildup in the body: kidney stones,
tartar on teeth." She teaches me all this
as I sit there with my mouth open,
looking astonished.

Repair

My wife's ex is up on the roof
repointing our chimney.
I can hear him walking around up there

as I lie here in bed thinking
about the symbolism. It feels
a little like he's walking on my grave

and a little like I'm sleeping in his. "He's very
handy," said my wife. "He can fix
anything." I suppose most men

would find it too emasculating
to hire their wife's ex-husband
as a handyman. But I am not

most men. And I am not
the least bit handy. As for their marriage,
that was something he couldn't

fix, not after he cheated on her.
And now the bricks are flying
outside my window, bits of mortar

and flashing raining down as he chisels
them loose. My wife is getting
out of the shower. I can hear her

humming to herself in there. Soon
she will stroll into our bedroom with
a towel around her head, her magnificent

nipples shining and a grave
mischief in her eyes as she begins
making love to me all morning

beneath the hammering blows.

Worcester

In Worcester, Massachusetts,
outside the Worcester Free Public Library,
there's a line of homeless people
waiting to freshen up in the library's
free public toilets. And the senior librarian
isn't happy about it. How many will borrow a book
when they're done in the toilets? she asks the junior librarian
who is returning a book of poems by Elizabeth Bishop
to the poetry shelf. Before she moved to Worcester
for the junior librarian job, the junior librarian
lived with her aunt in Greencastle, Indiana,
and didn't even know how to pronounce Worcester.
As for the homeless people, they aren't
happy about it, either. Some are heroin addicts.
And some are mentally ill. And some are both.
And some are neither. And some are here illegally
and trying to acquire English by distilling it
from the airwaves and the signage. And they would all
rather be reading their own books on their own
toilets in their own homes. Nevertheless, they love
the motion-activated faucets with sensors in them
where they need only hold up their empty hands to receive
the generous wordless warm egalitarian water flowing
over their wrists and palms and backs of their hands
like a blessing. And all of them, every last one,
would pronounce Worcester perfectly,
as a sort of benign library fine, if asked.

The New Criticism

My stepdaughter
says I'm boring.
"Everything you say
is boring and like
so seventies." Her mother
says I'm wonderful, though.
"She's being fresh. Don't
listen to her," she says.
But I can't help listening
because I want to be
fresh and not boring,
and I want to say 'like'
like my stepdaughter
because everything
is like something, not
exactly but sort of.
And she's so contemporary
and provocative and like
alive. She knows all the new
neologisms and would
never use *neologism*
in a poem. Like ever.

Poem

Some pronounce it *poim*.
Like it has an *oy* inside it.
The way an oyster
has an *oy* inside it. The way
all poems ought to have
a little *oy vey*
and a little *oyez! oyez!*
inside them.

Others pronounce it *po-um*.
Like it has an *um* inside it.
A thoughtful pause.
A caesura. A possum
that got run over,
its esses elided.

Me, I always say *pome*.
Like an apple or pomme
I want to bite into
because it has an *om* inside it,
a mystic and sacred
syllable I can't wait to reach
and I have no patience
for all the diphthongs.

My P.U.

Somebody, maybe Maria Callas, maybe
Sutherland, kept crooning, "*Mai piu, mai piu...*"
on the Welbilt radio in my grandmother's
living room. While somebody else, maybe
me, maybe my cousin Michael, had recently
farted. Never again would I hear that aria
(which was at least a hundred years old)
without hearing me and my cousin Michael
(who were at most eight and ten years old,
respectively) laughing hysterically, dying
operatically over and over again on the couch,
with that mortified diva confessing mournfully,
and that smell rising up as rich and sad as history.

Feckless

It comes from the Scots *feck,*
which sounds like an f-bomb
though it isn't an f-bomb.
Though it may be a distant
cousin. Go ahead, say it: feck-
less. Feels good, doesn't it?
You could try it out at home.
Say it to your father: "Dad,
that is totally feckless." And if
he says to watch your language
and sends you to your room,
you can bet your effing
dictionary as soon as your back is turned
he'll be looking it up himself.
And you will have taught him something.
And you will have taught yourself
to use feckless to good effect.
Which is still really the only way
to make a new word your own.
You have to give it to people. Pick
their pockets and give it back
before anyone looks up.

Visine

My left eye is killing me,
I say to my wife. It could be
allergies, she says. It could be
my retina getting ready
to detach, I say, or glaucoma
or syphilis or cancer. Why
do you always have to jump
to your death? she says.
I don't answer right away.
At the CVS, a whole aisle
of eye drops: drops for dry eyes,
drops for watery eyes, drops
for red and itchy eyes. My eyes
light on Visine and suddenly
I'm sixteen again and smoking
pot every day and trying to hide it
from my mother, cutting classes
left and right and writing
my stupid clever poems
about sex and trees and death.
There's a poem in here just itching
to get out, I think, as I tilt
my head back and squeeze:
two fat drops stinging as they go
to work. And how long before
Johnson & Johnson figured out
the reason for the precipitous jump
in sales? And how long before
I fell so far behind in high school
I ended up dropping out?
The truth is, I've been jumping
to my death all my life. Because
it's good practice, I say to my wife.
And what about your eye, is it
still killing you? she says. No, I say,
but now my feet hurt. And also
my right knee. That could be
from all the jumping, she says.

Bar Mitzvah Boy Considers the Lobsters in the Tank

I wonder if they suffer,
their claws tied up like that.
Like trying to yawn
with your elbows. Poor things,
I'd like to bust them out of there,
buy them up and let them all go
in the creek behind our house.
At $10.99 a pound,
and five dollars a week,
it would take me, let's see,
a pretty long time. That big one
climbing up on top of the others,
his foot in someone's eye—
what does it get him but closer
to the lobster pot? Better
to hide underneath or in back.
Be inconspicuous. Blend in.
Look out the window
like you're considering the weather:
tum-tee-tum. Even so,
they could call on you.
The world is like that.
But if you have the answer—
if you know your Torah portion
and your Haftarah portion
and all the songs and prayers—
you have nothing to fear. You can
sit anywhere. Hum a little tune.
Be conspicuous. Be idle. Be brazen.
When they call on you,
just start singing.
They'll praise you and maybe
give you enough money
to save all the lobsters.
Which would be a real mitzvah.

Elegy

All the lost time
spent looking
at the breasts of women

instead of the soft shapes
of clouds, the shoulders
of trees,

the jounce of a wave,
swell of the tide,

areolae
on a veined leaf
or insect's wing.

Benedict Arnold

"I did my report on Benedict Arnold
because those other guys were all taken
by the time I got home from my grandfather's
funeral in Florida. George Washington
and Thomas Jefferson and Benjamin Franklin
and Alexander Hamilton and John
Hancock and John Adams and John Jay
et al. were all taken and only Benedict
Arnold remained. Because nobody likes a traitor.
And his name is synonymous with betrayal.
The most infamous turncoat in our history.
But he makes for an interesting story.
And isn't that what history ought to be?
I mean think for a minute about what the man
risked. The punishment for high treason
for much of the history of England and its colonies
was emasculation, evisceration, and decapitation,
in that order. In other words, they would cut off
your weenie (excuse me, Mrs. Cunningham,
but it's true, you can google it if you want to),
then slice you open, and after you had finished
watching your intestines spill onto the ground,
they would cut off your head for good measure,
stick it on a spike or palisade, and there among
the other traitorous heads, display it for weeks
or months on end. For reasons of public decency
women convicted of high treason were usually
burnt at the stake instead. And that concludes
my report on Benedict Arnold. Any questions?"

Erica

Once upon a time I loved Erica.
I loved her name almost as much
as I loved Erica. She was tall
and athletic and had a distinctly
masculine way of walking
down the hall, holding her books
like a discus at her thigh the way
boys do, rather than an armful
of flowers at her chest like all
the girls. But it was the boyish ring
of her name, which comes from
Eric—though you didn't hear
the Eric in Erica until you saw it—
that really put the Erica in erotica.

Lion

The gazelles
speed by in their
huge metallic herds
on both sides
of the highway.
The solitary
powerful nomad
hunting them
with his radar gun
crouches behind
some trees in the median.
Out of the corner
of her eye she sees him
too late—his eyes
already flashing
in her rearview,
her heart leaping
like an antelope
pronking in her chest
as she flees among
the other antelope,
hoping it isn't her
he will outrun, over-
take, pull over
the rumble strip
to the shoulder,
his grille breathing
hot on her tail lights,
taking his time
writing her up,
her doe-eyed
hazards blinking.

Deaf and Dumb

The Deaf man in the waiting room
asks me how long I've been working
as an interpreter. I tell him
many years. Awesome, he says.
We sit there chatting, waiting
for the doctor to come.

He tells me a little about himself.
His parents and grandparents are Deaf.
His siblings are Deaf. His two young children
are fourth generation Deaf. The hereditary
master status of a kind of Deaf aristocracy
in the Deaf world. And I am duly
impressed. My turn to say: Awesome.

He is getting his Ph.D. in sociolinguistics.
His signing is graceful, fluid, symphonic—
like water everywhere seeking
its own. Chatting him up in the waiting room
is a pure joy, one of the perks
of my profession.

But the doctor is dumb about Deaf people.
In the little examining room
he doesn't address the Deaf man directly
but tells me to "tell him" this, "ask him" that.
The Deaf man notices, tells the doctor
to tell him himself, in the second person.
But the doctor doesn't know what the second person is.

He examines the Deaf man but he doesn't
see him. He doesn't look in his eyes.
He says to say "Ahh," but the Deaf man
refuses to vocalize, mouth wide open,
fists forming at his sides, uvula
hanging there like a punching bag,
silent and motionless,
while we wait.

Nothing to Say

He had nothing to say, he said,
adding only that saying so
was in itself finally beautiful and true.

That was his message. It was
something no one else had ever said
quite the way he was saying it.

Many thought they heard a quiet
sort of unexceptional wisdom in it
and nodded their heads in agreement,

nodded their heads to the music of it,
which wasn't an easy music per se,
not the kind you'd get up and dance to,

or beat a drum to, or hum to yourself
in an abstracted sort of way. But it grew
louder. So when his enemies and detractors

tried to silence him, they couldn't silence him.
Because he had nothing to say.
They could only scratch their heads and listen.

Privilege

Take, for example, the grass
in the suburbs of America,
how it forecloses the likes of
curly dock, tansy, clover,
creeping thyme,
buttercup, ragweed—
any raggedy brown
or blue or red or yellow
unruly thing
applying for entry here,
hoping to live and to flourish here—
all the so-called weeds,
all the beautiful wildflowers—
turned away, mowed down,
poisoned. And hasn't it always
been this way, only the pure,
cropped, decorous green
grass and its offspring welcomed here?
But at what cost to all of us
this skewed sense of beauty
and propriety, this monochrome
monoculture with its monotonous
traditions of separateness
and supremacy, totally lacking
in any flavor or utility
or spirit? The dispirited grass,
asleep in its vast bed
of privilege, dreams of the invading
hordes of color, riots
of dandelion, chicory, purslane,
which all make fine eating
and live on the other side,
out in the waste places,
out along the roadsides,
not very far away
but far enough away
so that the lonely, privileged,
uninflected grass begins to feel
a profound sense of loss
and a profound sense of sadness
to think of the fine company

and the fine eating
of its despised neighbors,
all the brothers and sisters
whom it has never met
and does not know at all.

History of Love

Because he loves the way she has
of touching him
and because she loves the way he has
of loving her
each has learned the other's
way and the other's touch
so when love turns
and the world turns
and the lovers turn from each other and go
to other lovers they take
they take all they know
of love and of touch
and they give it to another
and in this way love grows rich
and wise and wide among us
and in this way we are also
loving those who will come after
and those who came before
we ever came to love

Cleaning the Rabbit Cage

The round, brown, uniform, odorless turds
like diminutive canon balls piled
in a tidy corner

are identically unidentical,
no two exactly alike,
like snowflakes. I'm shoveling them

into the urine-soaked newspaper,
examining one and then another
between my thumb and forefinger:

individual, fungible, fudgy,
yet in the aggregate
a perfect whole, a dusting,

a few errant pellets spilling
onto the floor as I gingerly
remove the mother lode.

And what must he think, Pepper,
masticating in the opposite
corner, knowing enough not to

shit where he eats, even in such close
quarters? What must he be thinking,
he who always seems to be thinking,

chewing things over and over
with his two sets of incisors,
one behind the other,

seeming to pay me no mind,
yet surely noticing me here,
my head inside his cage,

harvesting his excrement,
as though I had a mind
to make something out of it?

Happiness

The dog isn't happy
unless his head is
sticking out the car window.

The man isn't happy
unless his head is
happy.

The man and the dog
have this in common,
thinks the man,

driving around with the dog
in the backseat, nose
in the wind, happiness

in the air.

from
LATE FOR THE GRATITUDE MEETING

(Kelsay Books, 2019)

Comma

There should be a comma here,
he said. And it made you want to
remove all the commas remove
all your clothes and dance around
naked with the poem in your hand
waving it around in the air singing
comma comma comma comma
while the other poets in the work-
shop clutched their pocketbooks
and pens and meh poems to their
caved-in craven chests your leap-
ing poem bungee jumping boing-
boing off the walls and ceiling cut-
ting the air with the cutting edge of
its lines like sickles like scythes like
live catenary wires whipping the dead
air of that bleak classroom kicking
fusty seemly sedentary poet butt
and you swinging from the killer last
line leaping singing windmilling right
out the door. But instead you said,
Yes, thank you, there should be,
and dryly inserted the comma with
your yellow-bellied number 2 pencil,
sat back and sighed with your slack
mouth open for more feedback.

Life Is a Banjo

Just ask the banjo players
and they'll tell you
they didn't choose the banjo
so much as the banjo
chose them—and now
they carry it around with them,
this conjoined twin
whose big round head,
pale skin, funny-looking
fifth tuning peg like a misplaced
thumb halfway up a forearm,
is part of them. Like
the body you didn't choose.
Like the life you didn't choose either.
Nobody gets to choose.
But you pick it up, you
dust it off, you put your
arms around it and you try
to love it. And you try to make it
sing. You get yourself
some fingerpicks and you
pick that damn thing like
the life you didn't pick
depended on it.

First Line

In the end of days what you need is a good first line.
To distract you from the truth with its own truth.
The way pain can sometimes distract from pain.
The way beauty can sometimes distract from pain.
The way a good bedtime story can light up the dark
side of an entire planet, given a little room
with a bed in the corner, a few right words, a child
listening. In the end of days what you need is a good
beginning. Something hopeful and trembling like a tongue.
Something open and unselfconscious like a mouth,
while listening to the words, and the music of the words.
Something steeply rocking like a ship, or a sleep, heavy,
floating, viable, smelling of saltwater and infinite possibility.

As It Happens

When they told me I was dying, which I wasn't,
I began to miss the things in the world which I didn't
even like about the world—the hideous traffic
on 95, for instance, which I found myself sitting in,
going nowhere on my way home, in no hurry now
that I was dying. I will miss this traffic, I thought,
feeling surrounded, girded, by people and life and
desire in the lanes. And the truck, the 18-wheeler
shouldering in, trying to pass on the right (I always
hated trucks), struck me now as a vessel of human
kindness, people helping people they don't even know
by bringing them food from far away. I will miss
all the trucks, I thought, as I rolled down my window
and waved him in, and gave him the I-Love-You sign.
I will miss the waiting, the fuming, the inching
along, the reductive bumper stickers and caviling
crazy drivers with their chutzpah and their daring.
And the road itself, which is every road, everywhere,
bending, unfolding, continuing on. Then I turned
the radio on and the talking heads were talking
about death—all of the deaths at home and abroad.
And I thought to myself, the living are talking about
dying but the dying are talking about living. I am talking
about all the living I missed already, all the living
I wanted to do—any kind of living at all—now that I was
dying, which I wasn't, as it happens, as it turned out.

Gray Day

It's the almost that I love
about a gray day
like today. In weather
like this, I almost
feel a kind of joy:
the heavy sky, the feeling
in the air of imminent release.
I feel like I could almost
cry. Cry as I haven't
since I was a boy.
Because I haven't let myself.
The overcast sky says: *almost.*
The charged air says: *could.*
You could do this.
You could let yourself go,
feel the thunderous sobs,
wave after wave, shoulders
heaving, lungs emptying
in that jagged way
that almost looks like
laughter. And the hiccuping
like a child that comes after.
It could feel so good,
says this feeling in the air.
Almost like joy, says the sky.

Bidet

The first time I saw one
sitting there next to the toilet
like the toilet's foreign-looking cousin
from Paris, showing up unexpectedly
on my trip to the hotel bathroom,

I asked my mother what it was for.
For washing yourself *down there,*
she said. And because I was only eight
or nine, and didn't know anything
about such things—Europeans or

their *down theres*—it turned into
one of those things that all my life
I have thought was for other people
but not for me. Like bungee jumping,
orgies, or visiting the queen. Fast

forward five decades: Last month
on a trip to Europe we met again—
me and the plumbing fixture. I stood there
in the hotel bathroom considering it
for a long time. You are nearly

sixty, I said to myself. Live a little.
And this is the part I want to tell you about,
the part my mother didn't have the words for,
the part that will make it or break it for
the poem about the bidet. Seated

on the toilet, I transferred my buttocks,
anus, perineum and genitals in one smooth
pas de bourree onto the bidet,
reached back for the soap dispenser
and the vertical jet, and lived a little

and loved it. I felt cleaner, fresher,
spryer. I felt like bungee jumping,
or making love to all of housekeeping.
I mean really. I mean royally. I am even thinking
of installing one at home. As a souvenir.

Late for the Gratitude Meeting

The guy in front of me in traffic
is letting everyone in,
waving at the cars like a policeman
or a pope—
and I really have no patience for all
the indulgence
and magnanimity at my expense

because I'm late for the gratitude meeting,
which is only an hour long.
And if I miss the first ten minutes
of silent meditation I'm going to scream,
because it's my favorite part and because
it helps me remember to breathe.
And I'm going to throttle this guy

if he doesn't stop deferring
to all of the trundling humanity
turning left onto Main
at this intersection where I'm fuming,
not feeling the love,
not feeling the gratitude,
feeling only resentment and disdain

because I have the right of way.
*Would you rather be right
or have peace? Let go,* I can hear them say
at the gratitude meeting three blocks away,
striking the rim of the Tibetan singing bowl,
which begins vibrating,
and keeps on vibrating,
like this steering wheel I can't stop clenching.

This Tree

I never noticed this tree before.
Was it always here?
Look how huge it is. Even the upper branches
as thick around as grown men—
strongmen in a circus with thigh-thick arms
holding up the canopy. You can't
miss this tree, and yet I think I've been missing it
for years, driving past it on my way to work
without seeing it. Now my car is
running quietly over there where
I pulled over because this tree
was standing here where I never
saw it. I see it now though. I see it all
now: How I couldn't see before because
of the understory—all those stories I was telling myself
were true. All the grasping and the wanting
and the dying. But now I think
there must have been something dead inside of me
if I couldn't see this tree. It's so
beautiful I want to die. I want to live
differently. I want to take this tree
back to my car, back into my life, keep it
always in view. But of course that's impossible.
That would be as impossible as this tree itself
being here and yet not being here.
Which is why I can't stop staring at it.

Feel Better

When I don't feel well I watch movies
about suffering. The Holocaust, the Middle
Passage, the Killing Fields. Any unimaginable
true story about people made to feel
worse than I feel now will do. There is no
lack of suffering. Why that helps me feel
better I don't know. It helps me feel awful
better, if that makes any sense.
Trying to make sense of suffering
only leads to more suffering—one can only
weep. To make himself weep, an actor
may bite down hard on the inside of his cheek
till he tastes the rolling boil of his own blood
mixing with the imagined pain. This usually does
the trick, and the world gets desolate fast.
And cold. So cold it makes you shiver. So fast
it makes you weep. And you reach for a tissue,
and you feel better. You feel awful, better.

Granted

You took it for granted because
it was. All of it. Every single
swallow required the work of more
than thirty muscles you didn't know you had,
let alone that they have names,
names you're learning now that you're learning
to swallow all over again. And to speak—
almost a hundred muscles involved in the act of speaking,
says the speech therapist, who visits your hospital room
daily since the stroke. And who knew?
Every little thing the body did,
every minute of your life, a friggin'
miracle of engineering. Every breath, swallow,
syllable. And now you're beating yourself up
for taking it all for granted. But what's given
is given. It remains given even if
you lose it. Even if you never get it back.
And if you do get it back—praise
the doctors and nurses, praise the speech therapist,
praise the unspeaking cashier in the hospital garage
half smiling a little sadly on your way out—
for God's sake, take it for granted
now that you know that it is.

Practice

You can't even let go
of the blue casserole dish—
how in the world
are you going to let go
of the world? I ask myself,
standing in my kitchen
in the late afternoon sunlight
which is turning everything to gold.
Everything, that is, except the blue
casserole dish, which isn't here
because my stepdaughter borrowed it
without asking me.
And it pisses me off because
I love that casserole dish.
Because it belonged to my mother.
Let it go, I tell myself, or maybe
that's my mother telling me,
because she had so little time herself
to practice letting go, suddenly
finding herself on the gurney
in Emergency, apologizing
to all the nurses: "I'm sorry.
I'm not very good at this." As if
"this" were something one could
get good at, if one practiced
letting go a little at a time,
practiced dying a little at a time,
practiced turning to gold a little at a time.

Roll Over Bell

When I see Deaf people signing into their smartphones—
singing into their smartphones—I can't help
thinking of Alexander Graham Bell,
enemy of sign language, oralist, teacher
of the Deaf, and inventor of the telephone—
the single greatest handicap
to Deaf people's pursuit of jobs and happiness
for a hundred and fifty years. I imagine him rolling over
with Beethoven, whose own deafness was variously
attributed to syphilis, lead poisoning, typhus,
his habit of immersing his head in cold water
to stay awake while composing. *Roll over
Beethoven, and tell Tchaikovsky the news,*
the Deaf are singing into their cell phones, signing
into their cell phones. *Signing is the most beautiful singing
the world has ever seen,* I whisper to Bell, who doesn't
see it. Though he can't stop staring. He grabs a fistful
of his own beard, as if to pinch himself awake
from this impossible dream he never dreamt because
of a failure of imagination. *Watson, come here, I want you...
to see this.* The dream that any Deaf
Tom, Dick or Harry, or John, Paul, George or Ringo
or Ludwig with two thumbs could punch in a number
and see the most beautiful singing the world has ever seen
and understand what it means—that dream is coming true.

Song for Bill

That was a lovely death.
Quick and clean and painless.
You've made us all jealous,
dying in your sleep like that
just five days after stopping
dialysis. Just two months after
deciding to do it. Time enough
to max out your credit cards,
sell all your stuff, give all the money
to your daughter who doesn't
have any money. I bought the 5-
string banjo, the wooden stool,
two hanging plants, the framed
calligraphed Whitman quote
about going freely with powerful
uneducated persons. And the clutch
of harmonicas. You told me
I better wash them because
"they probably still have my spit in them."
I haven't washed them. I hold one
up to my mouth, put my tongue
to the wooden holes. Inhale,
exhale. Lovely. Lovely.

White Lie

The snow covers up
the ugliness of the world
for a little while

but then it melts
and the world grows even uglier
because now it's muddy-ugly

which is like telling a lie
that leads to a truth
that is a starker truth

Reprise

I like to do things twice.
Reread the book I liked.
Watch the movie again.
Eat what I had for dinner
last night tonight. Have
another drink. Kiss her
one more time. Remarry.
Get another divorce. Make
the same mistakes. Learn
twice as much from them.

Danse Juive

The older I get the more Jewish I look.
I don't feel particularly Jewish
but I look like a Jew. Have you noticed
how some people dance around
the word *Jew*? They don't like to say it.
As if it sounded vaguely pejorative.
As if they only ever heard it used
as a verb. As if it were somehow
offensive to people of the Jewish
persuasion. But I am not persuaded.
I am not of the Jewish persuasion.
But I sure do look like a Jew
with my graying beard and famous nose
and curly hair and glasses. The older I get
the more people are dancing around me.
Everywhere I look these days
the people are dancing. And they're getting
younger and younger the older I get.
They're laughing and singing and dancing
around and around like they're doing the Hora
and I'm this old Jew in the middle
just standing here all alone like a verb
of being. Because I don't know the steps.
And I don't know the time. I don't
even know the words to the song.

Lesson

They kill the intellectuals first.
It goes back to the old hatred
for the smartest kid in the class,
the one whose hand was always up,
practically levitating in his seat—
"Oh, I know, I know." But he didn't
know they kill the intellectuals first.
Didn't know the stolid, bored,
back-row kids who were slow in school
would be swift and decisive
in violence. Where did they learn it?
he asks himself now, the blood
gushing from his nose and mouth,
the articulate fingers reaching out
from the sleeves of the well-ironed uniforms
to remove daintily, almost lovingly,
the eyeglasses from the blinking eyes
of the intellectuals first, then dropping them
to the ground, then crushing them
with the boots. So much to learn, dear heart,
say the ironical uniform evil smiles,
which, stitched together, form a kind of
horizon line at the end of the world.

The Case for Baby Talk to Animals

"Wittle Miss Paulinette is so bootiful,"
said Mr. Gordon, my high school English teacher,
as he combed her mane with his reader's
hand. All of Mr. Gordon's cats were named
for characters in Russian literature, Paulinette
for Turgenev's daughter. It was a little weird,
after hearing him hold forth in our classroom
on the great Russian writers for a whole year,
to hear him now in his living room talking baby talk
to one of his cats. And what would Mary Oliver
say? We were graduating in a week, some of us
were eighteen and legal, and Mr. Gordon had
invited us into his home for wine and poetry
to celebrate. The baby talk was disconcerting,
though Paulinette exulted in it, eyes closed, purring
worshipfully in his lap. "'Nothing in the forest
is cute,'" I said, quoting Mary Oliver. "We are all
wild, valorous, amazing. We are, none of us, cute."
Then I took a sip of wine, and set my wine glass down,
feeling like I'd made my case. Mr. Gordon said
he agreed with Mary Oliver, but that did not preclude
his talking to his cats in the only idiom other
than Russian (he did not speak Russian) that they
understood. And what they understood was
he loved them like his own children (he did not
have children), unconditionally, in spite of their
killing the occasional wren, titmouse, cardinal
at the feeder, which broke his heart, he said, more
than the tragic poems of Akhmatova. The cooing,
the high-pitched voice, the glissando variations
of his intonation when he spoke to them—this was
how he put into words his profound affection for them.
And if that embarrassed us, he said, it was only
because we were still too callow to understand love,
at least the kind of love great literature treats of.

Wild

None of it was worth your wild.
Your own feet, which are as good as
dead, wrapped in the shrouds
of your socks and lowered into the coffins
of your shoes each morning,
wouldn't know the earth if they were
in it. Which soon enough you will be.
You wouldn't know your wild if it was
right under your nose—and your nose,
which you have forgotten how to use
after a whole lifetime of disuse,
ought to be impeached, divested
of its privileged position at the prow
of your face, where it's been pointing
blindly forward all your life like a travesty
of navigation. Even your sex,
which you can barely glimpse anymore
for the portly promontory accreting
grotesquely above your nether region—
the region that is the very seat
of your wild, the soul of your wild—
has grown tepid, dispirited, tame.
Ask yourself, was any of it worth
your wild, now that your wild has flown
and you wouldn't know your wild if it was
your own face staring you in the face?

Caterpillar

after Ian Sanborn's ASL poem of the same title

A man with eyes as blank
as the indifference of nature
is staring straight ahead
as the whole thing unfolds.
He has a black beard, black
shirt, black woolen cap—
he could be a thief—you better
keep your eyes on his hands
which have begun clearing
a clearing. Here he plants
a seed as small as his own
fingernail, and shazam! it sprouts
roots, shoots, stems, branches—
a whole tree shouldering up,
tossing and swaying in the air
between the sun's magic hands
and the man's indifferent eyes.
Next thing you know, an orphan
index finger is worming its way
across the stage that wasn't
a stage until your eyeing it
made it so. It inches over
to the tree like a lost knuckle
finding its way home, its feelers
testing, feeling, sniffing, finding
purchase, finding a toe-hold,
the tiny, spiny, hairy, leg-like
appendages beginning to wiggle,
to climb, to shinny up the tree,
the elbow, the sheer escarpment,
pausing to send out a line,
a lasso, a long rope as fine
as the filament of a spider
launched from its abdomen
and hooking the thumb
of the lowest branch. A rope
for rappelling, for jumping off
this cliff, taking this dive,
twisting as it untwists, enfolding
as it unfolds, holding on for
dear life as it spins itself into
silk, those indifferent eyes
almost imperceptibly squinting
in sympathy with this closing up,

this cloaking, this cloistering,
this hanging upside down with
a pulse inside. A fluttering
pulse. A pulse like the flutter
of eyelids. Like the flutter
of wings. A heartbeat growing
stronger, stronger, breaking
out, breaking free, the wings
opening, the eyes opening as if
all this time they were closed—
the blank eyes opening to the
wings, taking them in, incredulous,
in love with them—and the black
and white has grown iridescent;
the orphaned knuckle has found
the hands; the hands have found
their wings, and we are all
utterly blown away.

from
MOSTLY

(FutureCycle Press, 2021)

Love Letter to Carl Sandburg

I'm sipping my tea on the ground floor
of the Federal Reserve Building,
a handful of suits at the table behind me
talking about profit margins, inventories,
low hanging fruit, when I notice this little girl
on the sidewalk outside the window,
conducting the wind with her tiny hands,
the autumn wind, which is counting its money
and throwing it away, counting its money
and throwing it away—a whirlwind of dancing leaves
going up and around and around in the wind tunnel
that this tall building I'm sitting in has created
with the other tall buildings. And as though
she had created it, she conducts it, shapes it,
urges it with her twirling hands
to keep counting its money and throwing it away,
counting its money and throwing it away
in front of the Federal Reserve, where now I see
her mother waiting at the curb with a big
suitcase and a little suitcase, texting,
scanning the intersection for their ride-share,
not looking at the girl or the swirling leaves,
looking only at her phone, and the endless line of cars,
searching for the one that's theirs. And when it pulls up
on the opposite side of Atlantic Avenue
she waves to the girl to come—now—hurry!
And the girl waves goodbye to the symphony of leaves
that goes on playing and dancing without her
as she pulls the little suitcase behind the mother
who is pulling the big suitcase toward the waiting car.
And I can almost feel you here, right beside me,
seeing what I'm seeing, wanting what I'm wanting:
to write it all down, not for the suits at the table behind us,
still talking about expenditures and revenues,
but for the wind that goes on counting its money
and throwing it away on Atlantic Avenue.

Going Back

It's not that I want to be young again—
God no. I wouldn't wish that on my worsted-
sweatered-old-man-in-sensible-shoes
self. I mean, we barely made it out alive
the first time around. But I'd like to talk to him—
that lonely, bored, back-row kid
I was back then. Because I think he would have
liked me. I mean, I think he would have liked
the way he turned out. And I know he would have liked
to ask me a million questions. Many of which
I know the answers to. I picture us sitting
on a bench in Taylor Park, one of his PF Fliers
jackhammering nervously next to my sensible shoes.
He looks away. Doesn't speak. I ask him if
there's anything he'd like to know. He looks up at me—
from this angle he can see all my ugly nose hairs,
thick as grave-grass. I no longer even bother
to trim them. "How old are you?" he asks me
and I tell him: 62. "Do you have any kids?" Yes. Two.
"Where are they now?" One is in New York City
and one is in Hawaii. "Do you miss them?"
Yes. Very much. But I miss you even more,
if that's possible. "Am I going to beat Marc Peo
in the wrestling tournament?" Now it's my turn
to look away. "That's OK," he says, "you don't
have to say it. I understand." And he puts his little hand
on my shoulder. "What about Cheryl Lubecki?"
What *about* her? "Well, do you think she likes me?"
I think your strategy of pretending not to be interested in her
isn't working. "OK, thanks for telling me." And he looks
away again. A long silence. The trees in the park,
which are much older than both of us, seem to chortle
in the breeze. Is there anything else you'd like to know?
He takes a minute to think. Then asks, "Are you happy?"
Oh yes, in fact (and I start to choke up a little) being here now
with you, I am happier than I have ever been in my life.

Wording

Every poem should have a bird in it —Mary Oliver

Cynosure, gravid, pabulum—
just three of the many
unusual specimens
I'd been lucky enough to glimpse
in the last few days.
And then at the dentist
I heard *risible* singing
from behind my hygienist's
face mask: "These muscles
around your mouth," she said,
"are your risible muscles,"
and I reached for my metaphorical
binoculars and feasted
on *risible* perched at the edge
of that noun phrase,
where I'd never seen it before.
It was a rare sighting and I could sense
the dinosaur DNA of that dactyl
going all the way back to the Old French *rire,*
and the Latin *ridere,* and maybe
I felt a little *ridiculous*
as I offered her my invisible
binoculars and she declined because
she was wearing a face shield
over her face mask, and her hands were full
of my teeth. Nevertheless, I know she appreciated
risible the way I appreciated it
when I heard its song—which sounds like
laughter—emanating from her own mouth
as I sat there with my mouth open
wider than song, wider than laughter,
as wide as a baby-bird mouth.

Indolent

"If you're going to get cancer
this is the one to get,"
said my radiation oncologist.
"It isn't the aggressive kind.
It's what they call the indolent kind.
Hell, you'll probably get hit by a bus
before you die of this thing."
And he looked out the window.
And I looked out the window.
There was a bus stop
across the street. But there wasn't
a bus. And there were no people waiting
for the bus. Nevertheless, it was a bus stop
the way the cancer was a cancer. It was
official. You could look it up
on the transit authority's list of city bus stops
and there it would be: #39 on the corner
of Walnut and Peabody. You could
go to radiation oncology and there
I would be: 51 with my cancer, the one
to get, the indolent kind that misses
the doctor's appointment
because it missed the #39 bus
because it couldn't get out of bed this morning
because it was having such a wonderful dream,
a flying dream in which, amazingly,
just by doing nothing,
by remaining absolutely still,
suddenly you're flying.

Sneeze

I love the benign
violence of it—
impossible
not to close your eyes
when this small
homemade bomb goes off,
unnerving
a few bystanders,
but causing no
injury or damage,
and then—incoming!—
a second explosion,
and maybe a third,
then a rickety lull—
itchy, intoxicating—
before the final
salvo, finale, sonic
boom! Clean
sweep. Mission
accomplished.
Knowing smiles
and blessings all around.
No need for alarm,
no return fire, no
casualties, no grieving.
Just clearing
the old nasal mucosa
of all the latest
foreign invaders,
thank you very much.

Grr

I love the grouchy words—
peevish, irascible, fractious—
I am all of them—crabby, morose,
snarky and more. I hate the phrase
"and more." It's so American, so
manifest destiny. I hate all the increase,
all the excess, all the productivity—
the abundance, the stuff, the shelves
upon shelves. And the free
shipping. We're prolific as fuck and I am
such an asshole. I'm surly, tetchy,
moody, nasty and gnarly. I admit it.
I revel in it. I'm querulous, captious,
and vindictive. And it's not just the adjectives I love.
I love the verbs too. Lour, glower,
growl and glare. And snarl. And more!
My stepdaughter gave me a T-shirt
with Grumpy on it. You know, Grumpy
of Seven Dwarfs' fame? I love it.
I own it. I wear it like a badge of
assholiness. Like a bellying flag. Listen,
don't be an asshole if you can help it.
But if you can't help it, help
others to understand the assholes.
Be an ambassador of assholes.
Wear it on your sleeve, on your chest,
on your boobs. Wear it on your belly.
Because you can't be what you want to be if
you can't be what you are first. So go ahead,
be that way. And if you don't love yourself,
try loving the superabundance of pithy words
for describing someone as hateful as you.

Vernal Scrooge

The hounds of spring are on winter's traces and I hate
a slobbering dog. All this mucus and affection
is making me sick, not to mention the ejaculations
of the junipers, oaks, alders and maples—I can't
stop sneezing and I'm all congested. The erectile
tail feathers of the wild turkeys—the way the males
display them proudly to the females—leave the females
unimpressed. I, too, am unimpressed with spring
and all its fecundity. I miss the white lie
of the noiseless, atoning snow; the brown study
of the bare, ramifying trees; the long, cold, invisible
diapause of the insects. I hate to be a buzzkill but
the bees aren't disappearing fast enough for me.
All these propagators and multipliers—the springtails
dropping their sperm on the ground and just waiting
for the females to come and pick it up—they can all
go fuck themselves. You can all go fuck yourselves,
you lovers of spring, you gardeners and joggers
and dogwood-huggers. I say there's too much sex
in the world, too much fruitfulness, too much seed
on the wind, too much pollen in the air, and much
too much begetting on the ground. I'm getting too old
for this. I'm staying in and counting the days till fall.

Talent

He played that thing all the time: waking, sleeping, walking, riding his bike, reclining in the bathtub fully clothed, where the acoustics were the best, he said. And in the backseat of the family Buick when we were trying to have a conversation up front. It was annoying. If we turned the radio on to shut him up, he simply played along with it, the squeaky little shit. It never occurred to us that he was on his way to greatness. One of the greatest harmonica players ever: jazz, folk, rock, Latin, blues, country, even classical. The inventor of the chromatic playing style on a regular diatonic ten-hole harmonica. But to us he was just the kid who sucked and blew and drooled a lot with that thing forever installed in his mouth, alternately buzzing like a beard of bees, chugging like a locomotive, wailing like a professional mourner, chiming like a bell, whistling like a blue jay, or a catcall, squeezing out the chords and major triads like an accordion, then bending one single note so low, so lonely, that it almost broke. Mom lost it once, screaming *Put that thing away! I can't hear*—she was on the phone—and she confiscated all of them (he had one for every key) for a whole week. He wept and begged her to give them back—*just one, please, I'll play quietly*—but she wouldn't relent. He cried and cried, emitting these strange low animal noises and high keening sounds as though he had a blues harmonica stuck somewhere deep down inside him and was trying to get it out. She hid them in the fruit bowl, under the apples, which she knew he never ate. I reached for an apple, glimpsed the shining underneath, the buried treasure he'd have killed for, and was dying without.

Anonymity

Remember that alcoholic you tried to help, the one you took to those meetings, those meetings you were attending yourself because you needed help stopping drinking and the only way to get it, they said at the meetings, was to give it? Remember those boxes he asked if he could store in your garage because he'd just lost his apartment and was basically homeless now? Remember how you made a place for them in a dry corner near the bicycles and Christmas decorations? Remember how he promised he'd come back for them soon, but then he stopped coming to the meetings and months went by and soon it was winter, the boxes huddled in the dark against the cold? Remember how you made it through the holidays without a drink, then asked around at the meetings but no one had seen him? Remember how you thought of looking online for an obituary but you didn't even know his last name—because anonymity, they said at the meetings, was the spiritual foundation of all their traditions? Remember when you decided to open the boxes—just to look for his name, you told yourself—and (Merry Christmas!) what you found were hundreds of albums and CDs: oldies rock and jazz and folk and blues, many of them rare and out of print? Remember how you carried them into the house and took them out one by one and made a list of the titles and listened to them over and over, over the next sober weeks and months, and by the time you celebrated a year clean and sober his record collection had merged with your record collection? And someone at the meetings said he was dead. Are you sure? you asked. Yeah, they found him frozen to death last Christmas in a snowbank. Remember the brief shock, and then the sweet relief you felt wash over you, thinking only of the records and yourself? Remember how that sweetness turned sour, how it started to burn, how you couldn't listen to the records anymore, the pleasure gone now? Remember how you ended up selling them all for a thousand bucks, then ended up picking up a drink, then ended up spending all the money on booze and drugs, then ended up back at the meetings, where the help was, the help you got by giving it away?

Barbershop

"Nobody calls it a barbershop anymore
except you, Dad," says my son
when I tell him that's where we're going.
It seems it's called CostCutters. And they're called
hair stylists. It isn't even called
a haircut anymore—it's called a taper, or a fade,
or a number two on top and a number
one on the sides. And there isn't
a coke machine by the door anymore
that sells coke in glass bottles. There isn't
a transistor radio up on a shelf anymore
with the ballgame on. There isn't
a red-and-white striped barber's pole outside Dominic's
with an old Italian barber named Dominic
who's been there all my life and probably
most of his life, pushing the long broom
a little closer to my mother, flirting with her
anymore. But some things haven't changed: they still
wrap you in a cape, and they still
look at you looking back at them in the mirror
as they stand behind you and ask you
what you want. And what you want,
though they call it something else now,
hasn't changed either—they still touch you
in a way that feels good, and they make you look good,
and smell good too, and you still walk out of there
feeling a little lighter, a little younger, a little closer
to beauty, though nobody calls it that because you're a boy.

Elegy

for all the
skinny
lovely
wistful
brilliant
brave
unread
poetry
collections
out there
with their
spines
leaning
left or
right or
maybe
posture
perfectly
straight
like our own
beloved
children
standing
at attention
chin up
chest out
name tag
showing
or else
horizontal
piled
supine
like the dead
like so
much dust
collecting
dust

Trump Inaugural Poem

"FUCK YOU" is a spondee.
"FUCK you," with the stress
on the first syllable, is a trochee
whose rejoinder is either
an iamb ("Fuck YOU")
or an anapest ("No, fuck YOU").
Poetic meter and poetic devices
are not only not boring, they're
basic as breath, relevant
as politics or sex. "The dick
in the White House is not my
president," is a good example
of synecdoche—that part of him
representing the whole of him,
who does not represent me,
who does not represent anyone
I know, who does not represent
anything I believe in—which is
not only a fact, a true fact, but also
a beautiful example of anaphora.

To the One Who Stole a Book at My Poetry Reading

Good writers borrow, great writers steal,
they say. I say it belonged to you already—
the sounds of the words, the spell of the words,
and the words themselves, they belong
to all of us. As do the silences. As does
the breath. Ours the air in the room, ours
the shared mouth where the words live,
ours the deepest listening. Listen, after
the reading, when they lined up to buy my book,
it felt a little like extortion: me taking their money
and giving them back what was already theirs.
Poetry belongs to everyone. And to no one.
Kudos to you for insisting on that. Thank you
for reminding me my poems aren't my poems.

To the People Who Don't Write Back

Maybe you haven't written because
you're still reading
and re-reading what I sent you,
giving it the kind of close read it deserves,
the kind a lover gives a love letter,
a Sumerian scholar gives a cuneiform tablet,
a reader of poetry gives a poem she doesn't
totally get but can't get enough of.

Or maybe you haven't written because
you're still writing, still
agonizing over the right words,
deleting the superfluous poignancies,
rethinking the commas,
looking for better verbs, discarding
sentences, whole paragraphs, then starting
all over again. Then again,

maybe you haven't written because
people don't write anymore,
let alone read. Letter writing has gone the way of
candlelight. They're shouting "short-form copy"
from the rooftops and the laptops. The mailboxes
are disappearing. And so are the letter writers.
And the English majors. And the English language itself
is shrinking at the same time it's expanding,

not unlike the universe. Plus, the children
no longer collect stamps, nor even know
in which corner of the envelope to affix them.
Maybe you haven't written because
there is death in the world. And evil and email
in the universe. Maybe you're dead.
Or maybe I haven't heard from you because
I'm dead. And just don't know it yet.

That She's Beautiful

is beside the point.
What was the point
of his saying that she's beautiful
in the context of
her poem? I don't care
if he's a Bollingen
Prize winner with ten
collections under his belt—
what's under his belt
is the problem. You can't
say to someone they're beautiful
in an undergraduate poetry
workshop out of context, out of
the blue, even if it's
true. "Beauty is truth
and truth beauty" is bullshit—
it's sexual harassment,
is what it is. The way he looked at her
while praising her poem,
"its shape, its movement, its
passion," as though it were *her* shape
and *her* movement and *his*
passion—it grossed me out. The guy
could be her grandfather.
And the way he phrased it: "May I
just say, Clara, you are a very
beautiful woman," as though
it were a question—which it wasn't—
as though he were asking
permission to touch her breasts
while in the act of touching them,
then quoting Keats like that, it was
disingenuous and disgusting
is all I know and all I need to know.

Poem at the Breakfast Place

The girl who rings me up at the breakfast place
is wearing a T-shirt that says BREAKFAST SANDWICH
in big letters across her chest. "How's the breakfast
sandwich?" I ask her, not looking at her breasts
because I am by nature a fearful and shy man
and because I like talking about things without naming them
the way you sometimes can in poems. "It's really good," she says,
and gives me a smile that says she doesn't
like poetry but likes this poem so far. "I would love
to have that breakfast sandwich every single morning
of my life," I tell her as I give her the money
for my Earl Gray tea and apple cruller. "Then you must change
your order," she says, misquoting the last line
of Rilke's "Archaic Torso of Apollo." I look down
at my cup, my cruller oozing apple, then furtively at her lovely young
torso. "Life!" I correct her as she hands me my change,
frowning at me now, not with displeasure but
concentration, like she's really trying to get this poem.

Writing Assignment

A platitude and a platypus
have one thing in common:
their first syllable,
which comes from the Greek
for flat. The resemblance
ends there. Because a platitude,
which is sometimes referred to
as a cliche, is nothing like
a platypus, which is sometimes referred to
as the duck-billed platypus.
Bill of a duck, tail of a beaver, feet
of an otter, the platypus
is no platitude. It's an original—
the sole living representative
of its family and genus. Write
platypuses, undergraduates. Be
original, be surprising. Be the venomous
mammal that lays eggs, figuratively
speaking, whenever you write
or speak. Don't be flat or trite
like a platitude. Be the flat-footed
platypus with a body so genuine
that early European scientists
thought it was a fake—several
animals sewn together. Don't be all
you can be; be everything you aren't.
Be sphinxian and alive for once
in your life. One page. Due Friday at 5.

Lost

I could do without the world.
Just give me a letter
about the world,
one that I could
fold up in a pocket
and carry around with me
in the world,
and take it out now and then
and pore over it,
and weep over it,
tasting the salt tears
as I fold it up and put it away—
a letter I've read so many times
I've memorized it,
so I don't really need
the moist, creased, crumpled
disappearing thing itself
in my hands anymore
because it's in my head now.
And yet if I ever lost it
I'd be lost.

Good Book

Sometimes you can't *not* put the book down
to save it, savor it, smile and shake your head
at just how good the writing is
in certain places, just how fine
the choices are in the uncertain
ways, the beautiful lost ways
you trust a good writer to see you through—

can't *not* put the book down
to look up a word you don't know,
or a word you once knew but can't
remember now, like a face you recognize
but can't say how you know the one it belongs to,
even as you find yourself falling
in love with that face, wanting to know it
through and through—

can't *not* put the book down
just to sigh, stretch, look up at the ceiling
and be in your body with the book closed
in your hand, your finger inside it holding your place,
the disappearing place where you've been losing
yourself—deliberately, deliciously, abstemiously.
Like very fine chocolate, just a little
at a time. Okay, maybe a little more.

The Thing Is

All the things that can go wrong with a body
could fill a book. Lots of books. A whole medical library.
But the thing is, there's no point in naming them here.
Names that are sometimes long and sometimes short,
sometimes Greek and sometimes Latin. And sometimes
the person who first noticed, studied, and isolated a thing
that went wrong with a body ends up giving his name
to that thing. And thenceforth the people whose bodies
have that thing are given that name for the thing they have.
Which is a nameless thing, really. Nameless as a thousand
dialects of pain. Nevertheless, people are sometimes
made to feel better when given a name for the thing
they have. At least it's a thing, they think. It wasn't just
in their heads. But everything is a thing before it is given
a name. Even the body you have, or, more accurately, *are,*
was a body before it was named. And it goes back to being one.
And that's all that's ever wrong with a body. That's the thing.

Premature Ejaculation

"I love you," he blurted on their second date
before they'd placed their order,
before he knew anything about her—
her middle name, her place in the order
of her siblings, her favorite color, season, author, aria,
breakfast food, ice-cream flavor, the name
of her cat, the name of her alma mater.

"You don't even know me," she said, feeling
more alarmed than flattered, folding
and unfolding her napkin while he looked
down at his lap, as though that's where
all his overzealousness had spilled out,
spoiling everything, the gum-chewing
waitress flipping her pad open, licking her pencil.

Good Cry

I hadn't had one in years. I was
due. But the question was
where to have it, where to
do it? "You could do it here,"
said my therapist, taking in the tasteful
prints on the wall, the braided rug,
the upholstered sofa and chairs
with a wave of her upturned hand.
But that would feel like taking a dump
in the middle of your office, I thought
but did not say. "No," I said, "I have to do it
alone." "But that defeats the purpose—
a good cry is better when shared," she said.
We both looked out the window then
at the gray day, the constipated sky.
There was a long silence. I could feel her
checking the time. It started to rain,
then changed its mind. "Our time
is up," she said. So I went and sat in my car
and did it. And the people passed by
beneath their umbrellas. And the sidewalk
moaned. And the street lights flickered.
I felt cleansed. I felt wrung. That night,
when I told my wife about it, she said
a little ruefully, she wished it was something
we could have done together. And she wept a little.
And I wept a little with her. Which felt good.
But the one in the car was better.

Authorized

The sign at the end of the corridor
says *Authorized Personnel Only.*

Are you authorized? he says.
I'm an author, I say. I have
authored. I am authorial.

Don't be smart, he says.
I'm not smart, I say. I'm
pretty average, really. A writer
writes. Period. And reads a lot.

You can't be here, he says,
his finger worrying his holster.

There is no verb "to be," I say,
in American Sign Language.
Which doesn't mean that Deaf
Americans aren't. Or that they don't
talk about being. And I hold up
one forefinger.

I'm going to count to three, he says.
And he holds up one forefinger.

Your forefinger and my forefinger, I say,
are two persons, two personnel,
two pronouns, two classifiers
in ASL.

Two, he says.

But that's classified, I say,
hoping it might disarm him.

Three, he says,
and I blow him a kiss.

Breaker 1-9, he says into his walkie-talkie,
staring straight at me. We've got
a nut-job here. Do you copy?

That's when I take out my hand-turned
red cedar pen, and I begin copying
this all down.

from
PITCHING FOR THE APOSTATES

(Kelsay Books, 2023)

Bicycles

Now I would rather remember life than live it.
I would rather imagine life than live it.
I would rather watch life going on from the sidelines
in a comfortable chair than stand in the midst of life
living it. And maybe that strikes you as sad
or perverse. And maybe I'm kind of a perv because
I'd rather watch some young people making love
than make love myself. And I would rather
read a poem about bicycles than ride a bicycle—I am done
riding bicycles. I am done making love. I am,
sadly, too old for that shit now. But I will never
be too old for the memory, or the thought, or the idea
of making love. Or the word *bicycles,* which is
as good a word as any, and better than most. In fact,
I want *bicycles* to be my last word, my dying word—
not *I love you,* or *bless you,* or *God forgive me,*
but *bicycles.* And the people standing over me—
if there are any people standing over me at the last—
will look at each other and ask if they heard me right—
"Did he say *bicycles?*" "Yes, it sounded like *bicycles*"—
as I lie on my deathbed remembering or imagining
riding our bicycles in a summer rain, then abandoning them
on the edge of a wheat field, and taking off all our clothes
because it was raining and we were already soaked
and hot and young and sweating—and running
naked through that field in the rain, and then, breathless,
sinking down in the field and making love. I don't
want to *be* in the field, in the rain, with the bugs and spiders
and rodents, the roots and stalks digging into my skin,
the itchy stems and leaves, a rat snake slithering past
and me freaking out and losing my erection—I just
want to remember or imagine those two overturned bicycles
abandoned on the edge of a field, in which we were young
and soaked and happy and making love, kickstands
pointing randomly up toward heaven.

Forsythia

Every year around this time
I think of that little boy
with the bright yellow hair

in that book my mother loved,
because she loved everything French,
and wanted me to love it, too. That book

was harder than it looked,
even in English. "What must I do,
to tame you?" asked the little prince,

a boy with yellow hair
who loved a flower, a flower a sheep
might eat if he didn't get home soon. And then

he was gone. My mother's
birthday was just last week, early spring, still cold,
some snow on the ground, that time when suddenly,

impossibly, there's yellow again: the yellowest
yellow there ever was. And then
in a few weeks it's gone. Or just

changed. Not yellow anymore but
green now, just like all the other green.
She's been dead for thirty years

and it was thirty years before that
when she first read that book to me aloud
before I could even read. I looked

at the pictures: a boy with yellow hair
and questions spilling out all over. A hat
that was really an elephant

inside a snake. And an ending
that was very sad, though he didn't die
exactly. He went home.

He loved a flower,
which made that flower unique
among all flowers.

The Story of the World

Praise the im-
provised, the im-
perfect, the jerry-
rigged, the jerry-
built, praise Jerry, who-
ever he was, a lands-
man after my own inept
broken heart,
which I keep trying to fix
with a little duct tape
and Elmer's glue.
Praise Elmer, praise
the tacky, tottering half-
assed job, the un-
professional, the un-
reliable, the un-
stable and unsound. Praise
all the safety pins
and paper clips
and staples holding the story
of the world together,
a story that doesn't hold up,
with its impossible plot
and vast cast of rickety
flawed characters,
every last one of us un-
believable.

Homegoing

And what if dying is like
that time I got out of school early
because I had an appointment
and I pushed open the heavy doors
and walked out into the day
and it was a beautiful spring day
or a late winter day that smelled like spring
and if it was fall it was early fall
when it's all but technically summer
and there was a whole world going on out there
and it had been going on out there the whole time
that I was stuck inside with time
and teachers and rules and equations and parsed sentences
but now here I was among the tribe
of the free and I could go this way or I could go that way
or I could just sit down right here on this bench
and look around at all the freedom
that was mine and also the work crew's
breaking for lunch beneath their ladders and also the woman's
pushing her stroller along the sidewalk and also the man's
walking his small dog and smoking a cigarette
and it belonged to the cars whooshing by with a sound like
the wind in the trees and the wind in my hair
and the wind all around me and inside me
and also above me chasing the clouds running free
and suddenly there was my mother
looking somehow a little different
in all her freedom and all my freedom
until she rolled down her window and waved
to come—now—hurry
because I had an appointment
which felt like a real buzzkill
and I briefly considered turning around
and walking away from her
and going off on my own somewhere
to be alone and free for a little longer
or maybe for forever
but then I realized there was nowhere for me to go
except home

Bess

She was wearing a white button-down shirt
with snap buttons, waiting for me
to unsnap them. But I was shy and she was
in the driver's seat. So she started unsnapping them
herself. She was 18 and had her own car already,
an old-fashioned Volvo named Bess. She had named it Bess
because Bess was an old-fashioned name. I was barely 16
and didn't have my permit yet, but I had permission
as far as the snaps. We were parked in Bess with the lights off
idling in a green place somewhere in the twilight
of my childhood. Its real name was the Volvo Amazon,
derived from the female warriors of Greek mythology. But I don't think
I knew that yet. And I don't think I knew
she wasn't wearing a bra. She'd already unsnapped
2 buttons, to show me how it was done and to show me
the little hollow between her breasts called cleavage,
an old-fashioned word that somehow also applied
to my busty grandmother living in Florida. I gingerly
unsnapped the third button. Someone inhaled audibly. Maybe me.
It felt like unwrapping a present that I'd only seen advertised
in magazines. Suddenly she unsnapped all the buttons,
impatiently ripping the wrapping paper right off.
"Thank you," I whispered gratefully, then just sat there
staring stupidly. Bess made a ticking sound
that filled the silence. It could have been
the spark plugs—you're supposed to replace them
every 100,000 miles or so. Or it could have been
the oil was low, or the valves were maladjusted,
or the drive pulleys were worn out. What did I know about
what was going on inside of Bess, in that moment,
16 years old, stupidly staring, something like time, ticking.

Cocksure

I haven't been sure of my cock since that day
it refused to stand up when it was supposed to—
which was the day we were scheduled to "do it"
one truant spring afternoon in my father's house
when I was 16 and Faith was 18 and naked
and cocksure and straddling me on the bed, whispering
"fuck me, fuck me." I'm not exactly sure why
it wouldn't stand up. It may have had something to do
with the age differential, or the vertical differential,
or the breathy imperative coming down from on high,
or the several weightinesses: There was the weightiness
of Faith herself, who wasn't twiggy, chafing and bobbing
on top of me; and the weightiness of the prospect
of losing my virginity; and the weightiness of her position
as the editor of the literary magazine vis-à-vis my position
as the diffident young poet whose exquisite death poem
had blown the entire literary magazine staff away
with its lively metaphors and imagery and weightiness,
which I borrowed from the weightiness of the dying
of my father, from colon cancer, only two months before.
It was his poem and it was his death. And the bed was
his bed—he had moved out of my parents' bedroom
when the pain got so bad he had to be alone—on which
Faith was alternately declaiming lines from my poem
and breathlessly adding the refrain "fuck me, fuck me"
while I lay beneath her, cock soft, in my father's
sickbed, dying to fuck her, unable to, wanting to die.

Sleep by Howard

My cat Howard
is good at sleeping.
He can sleep on the floor.
He can sleep on the table.
He can sleep in a chair on a pile
of poems. Right now
he's sleeping in the box
my publisher sent
with ten author copies in it.
When I took them out
he climbed right in
and went to sleep.
The box is small because
the books are skinny.
And so are the poems.
He wouldn't fit if he didn't
compress himself.
Poetry is compression
and Howard is a poem
filling a boxy form,
his long complicated tail
reaching around to his head,
the last line giving a nod
to the first, the poem
tidy, circular, compressed,
yet wild, leaping, carnivorous,
its sleep delicious.

Throwing the Books Away

"They smell like mildew," she said.
"That's the smell of great literature,"
I said. "I read these in college—my parents
read them, too." And I reached for a book
by Melville that I'd never actually read but
always meant to, opened it up and took a whiff.
"They smell like your parents," she said,
"who are dead and moldering, too. Let them go."
"You're killing me," I said, and dragged a forefinger
across the spines of several metaphysical poets.
"No," she said, "the mold and the mildew and the booklice
are killing you. I'm trying to save you."

So I packed them up in some large bins
and threw my back out trying to lift them
into the hatchback, which, let me tell you, hurt
less than when the used bookseller told me
he wouldn't buy any of them, couldn't sell them,
didn't want them. Then I tried giving them away
to the library, high school, Boy Scouts, YMCA,
but no takers. So I left them in the hatchback
and drove around with them for weeks, their dead
weight shifting this way and that like so many
dead poets tied up in the trunk. Soon the car reeked
of great literature. I developed a cough,
a nasty postnasal drip, and a rash that wouldn't
resolve itself. So I took them to the transfer station

and the single-stream recycling receptacles.
"We don't recycle books," said the recycling guy.
"But these are some great books by some great writers,"
I said. "OK," he said, "if you remove the bindings and glue,
and rip all the pages out, I can let you leave them here."
For well over an hour, dear reader, I ripped the hair
and guts out of greatness, and it felt like a desecration,
destroying those books just to find a place for them
in the world. But as the words of the towering dead
mixed with the things of this world—junk mail, milk jugs,
old calendars, pizza boxes, cat food tins, and all manner of
indispensable details—I began to feel, inexplicably, better.

Prison Poetry Reading

When we arrived
they took our shoelaces.
But they gave them back
after the reading. Something about
weaponizing shoelaces. Nothing
about weaponizing poetry.
An inmate played the violin
as we filed in and took our seats,
then one by one we read our poems
to the inmates and the inmates
read their poems to us. You could
tell the guards didn't like poetry.
The poetry was a kind of
punishment for the guards,
a kind of escape for the inmates
who walked right out of there
in the poems, barefoot and twirling
the shoelaces, skipping and holding hands
with the guards, telling the truth,
not the whole truth but
lots of tricky emotional truths
which you can only
imagine.

Interesting

"Interesting," says my wife's ex-husband
to himself ("He can fix anything,"
she likes to say. "Except for his broken
marriage," I like to say.) as he considers

the door jamb, the strike plate, the lock bolt
on the door he's installing in our kitchen
because, interestingly, we all get along now
and I actually like the guy, so I hired him

to do some carpentry. Because I can barely
open a door, much less install one.
"Interesting," he says again and I know
it means he's encountered a problem—something

isn't fitting, isn't level, isn't plumb. I'm sitting
in the room across the hall with the door open, writing,
wondering about the difference between
level and *plumb*. And also, come to think of it,

between him and me. I want to say "interesting"
the way he does. But what I usually end up saying
is "shit," or "fuck," or "I give up." I'm always
closing doors, it seems, either because I'm unable

or unwilling, or, worst of all, uninterested.
But he says "interesting" to himself, and that's
interesting to me. It means he's open
to what's in front of him. Like opening a door

and walking right on through while looking
up and down and all around with interest,
willingness, maybe even amazement, something
I would like to do but never seem to do

in life—I only do it in my writing. And the fact
that my wife left a man who can fix anything,
a man who stands at the threshold saying "interesting,"
for a man who prefers to sit and write about life

than live it—that never ceases to amaze me.

Wilkinson's Swords

Neither of us shaved yet—
we were just seven and five,
watching TV, when he said,
"I have to pee." And I said,
"I have to pee, too," because
I did, and because I did everything
he did, because he was older
and wiser, and a little taller.

We stood on either side
of the toilet, our tinkling streams
crossing. "Wilkinson swords!" he exclaimed,
an allusion to the crossed swords
in the TV commercial for men's razors.
We'd seen it a hundred times
because we watched a lot of TV.
I may or may not have gotten
the connection between the swords and the idea
of a close shave. But I got the connection
between the crossed swords
and the crossed streams. As sharp

as if it were today, that image
of the two of us peeing collaboratively,
seven and five, respectively,

laughing together at the bon mot,
aiming our little weenies into the toilet bowl,
artfully directing the flow
across space, across time, across
a whole lifetime of big and little ideas.

Commandment

You gotta love
all your little hatreds,
all your petty
annoyances (*annoy*
from the Latin *odium*),
for they have been
around since before Latin,
Old Italic, Etruscan,
Phoenician, Hebrew and every
other tongue—your little
hatreds have been
spitting on the earth
since the second fish
who walked on land
trod on the heels of the first,
and probably got into it
with the third fish, too.
There is such a rich
tradition of resentment,
grudge and kerfuffle—
and kerfuffle is such
a great word, you gotta
love it. You gotta love
your neighbor as yourself,
but if your neighbor is
irritating, try loving
all your irritations, try
getting in touch with
the oneness of their long
branching history, whose
latest leafy unclenching
florid blossom you are.
It's a numinous workaround
and you gotta love it.

Pitching for the Apostates

I didn't want to play for a losing team.
That was what it boiled down to.
I mean, the Jews got slaughtered,
annihilated—

everybody knew that. And as a kid
I was big into winning.
So I wanted nothing to do

with being Jewish. I stopped
going to Hebrew school. I boycotted
my own bar mitzvah.
I studied German in high school.

I married a lapsed Catholic and didn't
look back. Things went along winningly.
We celebrated Christmas and New Years.
We were Americans. We were Democrats.
We were Red Sox fans. My kids

never heard of the Four Questions
and they never asked why
I quit that team all those years ago,
though today they vaguely know
that I am still somehow vaguely

part of that team—I know it myself—
even though I don't
play for that team, don't root for that team,
wouldn't be caught dead
in the uniform.

Letters from Camp

I've been reading the letters I wrote to my mother
over fifty years ago from camp—she saved
them all. When she died I found them
in a shoe box in my 9-year-old hand and
voice. A hand so loopy and innocent I could
weep. A voice I know like the back
of a very small hand that used to be mine

and somehow still is. The recurring theme
is winning ("We won the baseball game, I hit
a homer." "We won the swim meet." "We lost
the tenis tornamint because it was windy and the ball
didn't go where we hit it.") And also sugar ("Send
more candy." "We had fribbles from Friendly's."
"Dinner was pizza and coke and desert was
choclit cake. The coke and cake were yumy.")

Winning and sugar. Sugar and winning.
And it occurs to me, though the letters stopped,
the same themes continued for fifty years: winning
at school, winning in romance, winning at work, always
the need to kill it, to destroy the competition. The sugar
that was alcohol, the sugar that was sex, the sweet taste
of every conquest. How despicable I suddenly am
to myself. Only the misspellings are endearing,
those phonetic, understandable, forgivable mistakes.

Striptease at the Ars Poetica

First I took off my coat
because I was hot
and then I took off my hat
because forty percent of your body heat is lost through your head
which is a myth
but I like certain mythologies
and I like certain hat hair
which is perverse I know but I'm kind of a perv
so I took off my scarf because it was itchy
and then I took off my gloves
because it's hard to unbutton your shirt when you're wearing gloves
and I wanted to unbutton my shirt
so I unbuttoned my shirt
and I took it off and twirled it around over my head
and tossed it through the air
the way they do in strip joints and in movies
and at weddings
okay maybe they don't do that at weddings
they toss bouquets at weddings
and they twirl napkins at weddings
but you get the idea
and when I got the idea I took off my pants
because when a man gets aroused
he has this inexorable compulsion
to show his erection to someone who appreciates it
the way he appreciates it
as though it were something he had made
with his own hands
which some erections are
so then I stood there steeply rocking
in a sea of aloneness
because I was utterly alone in the Ars Poetica
with no one to appreciate what I had made
so I took off my shoes and my socks
and I hung my left sock on my erection
like a windsock
that shows the direction and strength of the wind
I didn't make the wind but I made a windsock
or the likeness or the image of a windsock
and I stood there naked in the wind for a brief moment
admiring what I had made
because it was beautiful and true and it slanted a little
due to the diminishing strength of my erection

and all of a sudden I felt very foolish
all of a sudden I felt very cold
and alone and with no direction
so I removed the sock and I put it back on my foot
and I put my other sock on my other foot
and I dressed quickly and self-consciously
and stuffed my hat and scarf and gloves back inside my coat pockets
and then with my coat in one hand and my shoes in the other
I tiptoed out of there in my stockinged feet
and I only am escaped alone to tell thee

Best Listener

The dog of myself
walking the dog of the dog
through the dog of the world.
I've been talking to myself
a lot lately. Too much, probably.
I am my best listener. No one
hears me out like I do.
The dog of the dog stops, pees
on a tree, and suddenly
I have to go, too. "The good
stuff, too, is contagious," I say
to the dog of myself zipping up.
The danger, of course, which is
posted on the trail—Steep Decline
Ahead—is the more you talk to yourself
the more you begin to resemble
a guy on a park bench talking to himself,
eyes wild, fly open, gesticulating
at his own inscrutable privacies,
barking at the dogs of the people
of the world passing by.

Jacob and Esau

My bar mitzvah portion was the story
of Jacob and Esau and the lentil soup.
At thirteen I was as smooth as Jacob:
I had learned just enough Hebrew to read
that bit from the Torah aloud, impress the congregation
and get the money. It was all a kind of fraud—
I had no idea what any of the words *meant*.
I had never even tasted lentil soup.
And when I finally did, I didn't like it. The story
of Jacob and Esau and the lentil soup
and the blind father, Isaac, as it turns out,
is a story of fraud. And thirteen isn't the age
when manhood begins—that was the biggest fraud—
though it roughly coincides with the onset
of puberty. At thirteen I could count the number of hairs
that were growing down there: approximately
thirteen. I learned about approximate equality
in algebra class that same year: when any two quantities
are close enough in value that the difference
is negligible, you use the approximately-equal-to sign
with a squiggly, which looked like one of the curling
tender tendrils growing down there. So it all fit together
approximately. I didn't have a hairy brother like Esau
or a blind father like Isaac, but I was smooth:
practically all of my friends were hairier than me.
I knew this because of gym class and because of
peripheral vision. I pretended not to see, but I saw.
I saw I would be a late bloomer. I saw that lentil soup
was an acquired taste. I saw I wouldn't start liking it
until many years later, when I'd grown enough pubic hair
to sport an excellent beard. A beard is technically
pubic hair on your face—any hair that wasn't there
before puberty is technically pubic hair, a factoid
that I thought the rabbi might appreciate. So I told him
during one of our boring weekly bar mitzvah lessons.
He made a face like he had indigestion, then fondled
his pubic hair and told me to keep reading. Just keep reading.

Do

for Dooder

"I'll do the portobello omelet
with bacon and swiss," says my son
to the waiter. And when the waiter leaves

I say, "*Do*? What happened to *have*?
You aren't going to *do* anything—
they're going to *do* it in the kitchen
for you. Then you're going to *have* it."

"Dad, the language is changing,
dude. It's alive. People say *do* now.
All my friends say it. You can say it, too."

"I will never say *do*," I say.
And he shrugs as if to say *have
it your way.* Then he checks his phone.

"Do you have to always be doing that?" I say.
"Doing what?" he says.
"That," I say, pointing at the phone.
"Can't we have a normal conversation

the way normal people do?"
"You just said *do*, Dad. You're
such a doodad." And smiling triumphantly,
he puts his phone away. And gives me my due.

Fishing Vest

I don't like fishing.
But I like hyperbole.
It had a hundred pockets.
I saw it in the window
of the sporting goods store
and I thought: now every poem
shall have its pocket. And I thought:
let there be plenty of pens
and pocket combs, a pocket
dictionary, a box of raisins,
a pocket watch, a deck of cards,
and a pack of cigarettes.
I like a poem that can hold
numerous small swindles
and lots of harmonicas,
a childhood memory
of an imitation turd
from a novelty shop
on Hancock Street. I hadn't
smoked in years, but now
I wanted a pack of cigarettes.
And I wanted a deck of cards.
I didn't want to go fishing.
I didn't give a shit
about fishing. What I wanted
was a poem that could hold
everything. Everything I wanted
and everything I didn't want
but was dealt anyway.
I wanted those pockets.
A hundred of them.
And the one that got away.

Quits

Let's call it quits. Let's take
five. No, seven, in honor of
the seventh day. No, in honor
of the cigarette, which takes
exactly seven minutes to smoke
all the way down. Let's call it
a day, a week, two weeks. Let's
take a liquid lunch and not
come back for days, weeks, months.
Let's not and say we did. I used to
say that a lot as a kid: Let's not
and say we did. It sounded
subversive and anarchic. I was
big into anarchy and subversion.
I quit high school and landed on my feet
in a college for creative fuck-ups
on the Hudson. I quit marriages
and landed on my feet in other
marriages. I'm all for quitting.
Quitting gets a bad rap. The people
who tell you to never give up,
to keep fighting no matter what—
don't you just want to slap them?
A few of them are standing around
my hospital bed right now, saying
to keep fighting. I want to get up
and slap them, one by one, then
hug them, hard, then lie back down
and call it quits.

Those Meetings

Are you still going to those meetings?

Those meetings are like no meetings you've ever attended
they always start on time and end on time
and everyone introduces themselves before they speak
so that no one forgets who they are or what they are
and they don't interrupt each other or even address each other
they just go around the room and tell these stories
and the stories are true and they're all the same story
with slight variations in the precious indispensable details
and everyone thanks each other in a chorus of thank-yous
and no one takes minutes and there are no action items
because everyone's action item is the same action item
and they do it together and they do it alone and no one
checks to make sure it got done and no one checks
to see who belongs at the meetings and who doesn't belong
because everyone belongs if they say they belong
and they can't kick you out unless you're disrupting the meeting
and in that case they do it gently and invite you back
and there are morning meetings and lunchtime meetings
and nighttime meetings and beginner's meetings before the meetings
and there are no executives and there is no meeting agenda
and they take turns running the meetings which always run smoothly
and everything always gets done that needed to be done
and everything always gets said that needed to be said
and they'll tell you there's no such thing as a bad meeting
and if you think your meetings should run more like those meetings
if you think your work meetings or town meetings or city meetings
or state or country's meetings should run more like those meetings
if you think the whole world should run more like those meetings
the people who go to those meetings won't disagree with you
but they won't be interested in extrapolating from those meetings
how to run the world because they're not trying to change the world
they're only trying to change their minds about the world

The Curiosity Factor

Don't you love that it's a thing,
the wretchedness
on the other side
spilling over, puddling
like transmission fluid or
blood, forcing us to slow down
because it's all so irresistible,
so infectious that we can't
look and we can't stop looking
at the beautiful catastrophes—
beautiful for the way they
bring us together over them—
in a world where every last one of us
is stuck here with no idea why,
hoping and praying it'll all become clear
somewhere up ahead,
the unseen hands of angels
bearing brooms, bearing stretchers,
and wreckers with winches,
not exactly clearing it up
but clearing it away somehow
before we ever get there,
so we never know in this lifetime
what it was we were waiting for
or the reason for our long suffering.

Nightmare

You're attending a reunion
of all the people
you've slept with in your life—
it isn't a large number,
less than legion, more
than minyan, a number
divisible only by itself and you.
It's a formal gathering in a room with
large upholstered chairs
and potted weeping figs,
a small bar in the corner
where two women you don't recognize
are seriously kissing, holding their drinks aloft
like tiny sloshing mountain lakes
in their slender raised hands. You aren't
dressed for the occasion,
you realize as you look down
at your ashy underwear and ten
poor stubby toes. It seems
you're expected to make a speech
which everyone has traveled far
through time and space to hear. You're
unprepared. No script. No notes. You
haven't even given it a thought. Now
you frantically ask one ex-lover
after another for a writing utensil. You
actually say "writing utensil" the way
your teacher said it in the 3rd grade.
No one has a pen. But someone
has an eye liner pencil. Now for
some paper. You're holding a damp
drink napkin in your hand, shaking it
in the air to dry it. If only you
could write, you think, maybe
you could still make something out of this
nightmare, something beautiful and true.

Affiliation

I was reading this cat research—
new research about cats—
that said we don't really know cats;
there are 58 million pet cats in America
and we don't really know them.

It said they don't like their cat food bowl
near their water bowl. Who knew?
So I moved my cat's water bowl
into the other room. He looked
nonplussed, then rubbed up against my leg
and gave my shin a headbutt.

Previous cat researchers, said this cat researcher,
have hypothesized that cats rub up against you
to mark you with their scent. That's balderdash,
said this cat researcher. It's really their way
of affiliating. I liked the sound of that—
affiliating. I also liked the sound of *balderdash*.

Affiliate comes from the Latin
'to adopt a son.' *Fillius* is Latin for son.
No one knows where *balderdash* comes from.

Now when my cat rubs up against me
or gives me a headbutt,
I know he wants to affiliate. "You wanna
affiliate?" I ask him in that baby talk
that cat lovers use with their cats
that annoys everyone else including other cat lovers.

I adopted my cat from the animal shelter.
But the research isn't clear, said the cat researcher,
exactly who is adopting who, with all this affiliating
going on. Fifty-eight million and counting.
I pick him up and we affiliate. He sits in my lap,
wise and regal, keeping his own counsel
and dignity, while I babble on in baby talk.

Landmark

My mother's new house
was the third house on the left,
the one with the big rock in the front yard—
you couldn't miss it. This was
on the third rock from the sun, the one
with billions of people on it—you couldn't
leave it, not even if you died
three months after retiring and moving to Boston
to be closer to your grandchildren. It was
a nondescript rock, a boulder really,
that the builder probably decided on a lark
to leave there: a sort of lawn ornament,
a sort of landmark. Sandstone or limestone
or maybe shale. She'll have a hard time
selling it with that rock in front, said my wife.
She won't sell it, I said. She's not leaving.
She died three months later, suddenly, unexpectedly,
a bacterial infection that overwhelmed her overnight.
We never found out how she got it. There are
more bacteria living on your skin
than people living on the third rock from the sun.
My son liked to climb it when we visited.
He was only 4. His sister was 2. They don't
remember the rock and they don't remember
my mother. The buyer said he didn't like the rock
but it wasn't a dealbreaker. The two of us
stood in the front yard negotiating. I told him
it was a great landmark—you couldn't miss it.
I told him my kids liked to climb it. I told him
my mother lived here only three months—she hadn't even
hung her pictures yet. Suddenly, unexpectedly,
I started to choke up. He put his hand on my shoulder
to console me, this stranger, this buyer, a tender
gesture that only made it worse, and I began to sob
uncontrollably. I hid my face in my hands
and turned away from him, and faced the rock.

Old Basketball Hoop

This abandoned post
on the edge of the driveway,
holding up the backboard and the rim
for more than twenty years now
in the same rusted pose,
like a monument to my children's
childhoods, which I pass beneath
every day on my way to work,
this memorial to H-O-R-S-E,
and Around the World,
and *nothing-but-net,*
a metal net that went ka-ching,
a sound so rich and gratifying
whenever we scored a basket,
and it still tinkles softly
when the wind blows through it,
though no one has taken a shot
in years. The whole contraption
with its frozen posture
reminds me a little of myself—
still holding out, still holding up
the circle of an empty embrace
for those same children
who are done being children,
who have moved away and won't
be moving back. It's a little sad
and a little ridiculous, frankly,
that a whole sandbox of sand
that once upon a time I poured
into that hollow base—
so the whole thing wouldn't tip over—
is still sitting quietly inside
just waiting for those children
to come out and play.

His Last Poem

It was just a tiny thing,
a handful of unrhymed couplets

about the warm tears
of old men,

tears that bless everything,
help nothing, no one—

each line like an empty clothesline
with a few orphan clothespins,

no clothes, no colors flapping
in the breeze. Just the sagging

line with its suggestion of a house
on one side, a tree on the other,

or two trees and no house—
then the clothespins flying away.

from
PERFECT DISAPPEARANCES

(Kelsay Books, 2025)

Golden Rule Revised

I hate
the part of me
that hates.

It's only
a part of me—
apart

from that part
I am loving
and kind—

but still,
it permeates
the whole.

I have tried
loving
that part of me,

but that backfired—
if you love
to hate

you will hate wholly.
No, the only
way to restrain

the part of you
that hates
is to hate it.

You must hate
yourself
as you would hate others.

The Heart Is Hard to Find

When I got cancer I got a gun.
Because my father had cancer.
And he didn't have a gun.
And he didn't have a choice
but to let the doctors shake their heads
over the mutilated remnant
of his life—which they had mutilated
in their vain attempts to save it.
First they cut him open and took some things out,
and then they moved some other things around
so he had to shit in a bag after that.
This is no way to live, he said before he died.
He died when I was a kid,
and now that I have kids myself
I wonder: if my father had a gun
and if he had the balls—if one morning
when my mother was at work and I was at school
he got out of bed and in his gray bathrobe climbed
the little hill with the overgrown rock garden
that was our backyard
and sat down on a rock, just sat there
for a long time with the gun in his hand,
a long time being of course relative—
half a minute is an unbearably long time
when you're holding your hand over a flame—
thinking, perhaps, about me and my mother,
or perhaps just thinking about whether
to put the gun in his mouth or to his temple
or to his heart—because the heart would be less messy
but the heart is also hard to find—
feeling around for it with his left hand
on the left side of his chest, listening with his palm
for his own heartbeat, finding it,
then with his right hand
pointing the gun between the fingers
of his left hand over his heart,
taking aim like that and then
fucking doing it pulling the trigger killing himself
in his own backyard because
this is no way to live—
I am wondering now, if he had died like that,
would I ever have forgiven him?

Frieda

Nobody wants to hear a white guy going on about
all the Black people he has known, especially not
a white guy who hasn't known many Black people,
and especially not the first Black person he ever knew,
the live-in maid in his grandparents' house
whose name was Frieda, Frieda Farrell,
who did the laundry and the cooking and the cleaning
and the clearing, and served the food at his grandparents' table,
and came from Jamaica, and came from Newark,
and came when his grandparents called her
with a little silver handbell from Germany
that they kept on the dining room table next to their plates.

And nobody wants to hear him going on about
how Frieda would come when she was called,
walking slowly, limping a little (she was as old
as his grandparents, maybe older) into the dining room
from the kitchen where she ate her meals alone;
how the bell would ring and she'd put down her knife and fork
and enter the dining room in her uniform, a gray and blue
livery, and stand beside his grandmother or his grandfather
and wait until they spoke to her. And nobody wants to hear
how his grandparents kept a collection of those handbells
on a shelf above the sideboard, all of them silver and ornate,

or how he remembers picking one up and examining it,
admiring its heft, the craftsmanship of its carved wooden handle,
when suddenly Frieda came limping in from the kitchen
because he had called her. But he hadn't called her.
He hadn't meant to call her. He would never
call her or anyone with a little silver handbell. "Don't
play with that, it's not a toy," she had scolded,
then turned and limped back into the kitchen. Nobody wants to hear
how he can still hear that little handbell he never meant to ring,
how it goes on ringing in spite of what he means or doesn't mean.

Grounded

When I was little
and closer to the ground,
I spent a lot of time
on the floor. Sitting on the floor,
lying down on the floor,
crawling around on the floor
and playing with the cat
who was closer to the ground
than I was. I was
intimate with carpeting,
its smells, the soft scratch of its nap
on my cheek, the faint stains, fallen crumbs,
chair legs, table legs, heat registers,
a dead fly, dried husk of a bee,
corners, baseboards. The older
and farther away I've grown
from the ground, the more
I have forgotten the view
from down there. Now
I'm all up in my head all the time
and the only time I get down
on the floor is to look for the remote,
or to play with the kids. Grown-ups
mostly don't get down on the floor
if they can help it. But soon enough
we grow old, we fall down,
we have accidents, strokes,
heart attacks, and we find ourselves
suddenly on the floor again.
I hope when my time comes
I will remember to open my eyes to the infinite
ingredients of dust, endearing
dirt, scuffed shoe, imperfect
stitching of the welt, loveable
ankles of the living.

Diminutive Wildernesses

He was my best friend in 2nd grade
and 3rd grade and maybe 4th grade too. I don't remember
when it happened exactly, but he had a sledding accident
at the bottom of that hill we called Bunker Hill
in somebody's backyard, and I don't remember
why we called it Bunker Hill or who came up with that name,
and it may have been the other hill,
the adjacent hill, the one we called Devil's Pit,
and it's possible it wasn't even somebody's backyard
but one of those diminutive wildernesses
that grew between the backyards and the houses in my one and only
childhood. But he was my best friend
and then he had that accident and then
he was in the hospital for a long time because I think he broke his neck,
which was something people said, like *careful you don't break your neck,*
but I think he really did and I don't
remember visiting him in the hospital and I don't
remember what happened to him after that—
I think he may have gone to another school,
a school for kids in the hospital
or a school for handicapped kids, and I think I remember
seeing him once in one of those neck braces—
I think they call it a halo brace—it was screwed to his head,
but I could be imagining that because what I imagine
has completely overgrown what I remember,
the way a diminutive wilderness will overgrow
and swallow up a house where no one has lived for years.

Years later, I googled him and found him online.
He's an orthopedic surgeon now with a thriving practice
and gray hair and a neat beard in that photo of him on the hospital website.
And I emailed him through the website
and asked him if he remembered me.
I reminded him that we were best friends in the 2nd grade.
I asked him if he remembered what happened exactly,
how we had lost touch and wasn't it good to be in touch again?
But he didn't reply.
But I didn't give up because I had so many questions,
because we were best friends, so I emailed him again
and asked him about the sledding accident
and if it was what inspired him to become an orthopedic surgeon,
and he didn't reply again, and after a third email and no reply
I called the hospital and left a message for him.
I finally got a reply. It was short.

He said he preferred not to engage with me.
He used the word *engage.*
I was puzzled, angry, hurt.
I tried to remember what happened but I couldn't remember.
And now I think it's possible that maybe I abandoned him—
I mean after the accident I don't remember but I imagine
that maybe I didn't know how to be with him,
because he couldn't come out and play,
because he was in traction and he couldn't move,
because he had broken his neck,
which wasn't just something people said but something that happened to
      people,
and maybe that freaked me out and maybe I stopped
calling him, and maybe I stopped being his friend.
I really don't remember.
But I imagine he remembers.

Window

The doctor said what I have is called
pericarditis—inflammation of the pericardium,
which is the lining of your heart.

"We can cut a small hole—it's called
a pericardial window—to drain the fluid
around your heart and lungs. It's heart surgery

but in the world of heart surgeries
it's only a minor operation." It didn't
feel minor. The drainage tube hurt

like a motherfucker. I was in the hospital
for ten days and during that time I had plenty of time
to think about what it means to have

a window in your heart. The doc was less interested
in the figurative than the literal. He gave me
an incentive spirometer to take home.

An incentive spirometer is a device for improving
lung function. You're supposed to breathe into it
slowly and deeply. It looks like a cross between a bong

and a musical instrument. I already wore
my heart on my sleeve and now I was walking
through the world with a window in my heart.

I had a glass bong when I was a teenager,
back when I was in love with Faith Roffman,
the first one to whom I gave my heart.

She broke up with me for Mark Winkles
who could play lots of musical instruments
including the saxophone. That hurt like

a motherfucker and it felt like I couldn't breathe
as I walked around with a hole in my heart
for weeks, months. I got high all the time after that

and turned into a real pothead. I tried quitting—
swore it off by throwing the glass bong on the ground
which broke into a million pieces—but the next day

I bought another bag of weed. All these years later
in my convalescence, sucking on my incentive spirometer,

I'm thinking about Faith. I want to tell her

about the window, how it's possible to look
back and have these fond memories of the pain,
to smile warmly at the suffering. I want to tell her

about the strange alchemy
that turned my first broken heart at sixteen
into this cherished thing I caress like a polished stone

in a pocket, taking it out often, looking it over
fondly, turning and turning it
in the light of today.

Tassel of Wheat

That art teacher back in 7th grade, what was his name, Mr. Pessolano, I was thinking about him recently because I had the radio on and that Hall & Oates song "Sara Smile" came on, which is a great song, and I was singing along with it and then I was remembering this girl named Sara who was in my art class with Mr. Pessolano in the 7th grade, or maybe she was in 8th grade because I think she was a year or two older than me, but this was in junior high back when it was called junior high and 7th, 8th, and 9th graders were together in one school and Sara—I can't remember her last name—was pretty and a little goofy and she could draw Goofy as good as Disney and she never wore a bra, unlike the other older girls, and she was a really good artist, I mean she was talented, I mean she could draw people and animals and cars in this cartoon character way that was really impressive and I wondered whatever happened to her and then I remembered this pen-and-ink drawing I did in that class—it took me weeks, months—of a tassel of wheat, very detailed, all the florets, like hundreds of them on a single tassel of wheat and Mr. Pessalano said to take my time and draw each one, give each floret its own time and attention with that pen he let me use, which was a special kind of pen, a pen-and-ink pen, and I did exactly as he said and it turned out pretty damn good if I did say so myself—a tassel of wheat contains pollen grains which are the male genetic material that fertilizes the ovary of a kernel and we learned about that in science class that same year, all about anthers and ovaries and I knew enough to know that Sara had ovaries and of course she had breasts that you could almost kind of see behind the cloth of her stretchy shirts because she never wore a bra and I couldn't look at them and I couldn't stop looking at them and then I was thinking you know I may still have it somewhere in an old box in the garage, that drawing I did in the 7th grade, which was pretty damn good, hell it was great, and then I was thinking how all children are great artists, how I was a great artist myself once and how sad it is to grow up and grow out of greatness and I wondered if Sara was making a living somewhere maybe as a cartoonist, because she was great, and I tried googling her but without a last name the keywords Sara, great, cartoonist, goofy, Millburn Junior High, braless didn't bring anything up.

Emu

I dreamed you the emu at the zoo.
The sign said you bit, but you blinked
so sadly. You had

no hands. You looked
flabbergasted to be there.
Speechless for the first time in your life.

You could only cock your head in that birdlike way
and bite the wire mesh with your beak, but I knew
the word you were trying to say

was *mistake.* Your favorite word
in the whole world. But there was no mistake.
After all, this was *my* dream. I was having it,

and I wasn't having any of your
biting, supercilious,
inventory-taking editorial

in my dream, I said
in my dream. Then I moved on
with my fistful of corn

to the fallow deer
who are always more timid
than hungry.

Over the River and Through the Woods

Drove all the way out to my grandmother's house in South Orange the other day, after some business in Brooklyn, just to have a peek—she'd been dead for thirty years and I'd been living up in Boston for longer than that—and though the house looked pretty much the same as I remembered it, there was now a sign out front that said St. Paul's Catholic Outreach. Something possessed me. I walked up the long driveway and rang the bell. A young novice answered the door and I told him my grandmother used to live in this house, that I remembered coming here for Shabbat dinners when I was a kid, and would he mind if I had a look around? He was very gracious about it and introduced me to the priests and other novices who lived and prayed in the house together and helped each other with things like "discernment." Which I misheard as "the sermon." "You help each other with the sermon?" I asked him. And he said, "No, with discernment." And I said I knew the word but wasn't sure how he was using it. And he said it meant helping each other to discern the voice of God as opposed to your own wistful, wishful thinking. And I didn't know what to say to that, so I said, "Hey look, the mezuzahs are still here in the doorways where my grandfather installed them," which wasn't a total non sequitur, and then they gave me the tour of the house which basically still looked the same as it did all those years ago because they hadn't done any renovations, maybe because the Church couldn't afford it, or maybe because of the vow of poverty and all that. The bathroom still had the same pink and green tile that I guess was in fashion back in the 1960s. It was a real blast from the past to walk through that old house where I hadn't set foot since I was a kid, and in the front hallway, where there used to be a large ornamental mirror with a gilded frame that me and my cousins used to pull faces in, there was now a simple, unadorned wooden cross. But I was pretty sure I could discern the shadow of that big old mirror, the shape of it, like a picture-frame shadow that's left on the wall after the picture has been removed.

Passage

The book I'm reading now my mother read
and loved. You can get this close to the dead
and no closer. I like to imagine her smiling
or sighing over this passage, the marginalia
like lichen on a stone between the name and dates
and words from scripture. Her face is frozen now,
inanimate as the verdigris-covered headstones
in the cemetery I never visit because she isn't
there. She's here, in this book she loved—I can almost
see her gaze on the page, a faint patina covering
everything. I wonder what she said about this book
when she got to the last sentence. And if there was anyone there
to listen. I wasn't. There. And I wasn't listening. Away
at college, I wasn't reading much either, though I was allegedly
majoring in English literature. Mostly I was drinking
and smoking and making love or trying to, and feeling
motherless and existential. When she called I talked little, half
listening, scribbling on the wall beside the payphone.

Rethinking Rodentia

He pulls up in his pickup,
the names of rodents written
in an elegant cursive
that scrolls across the driver's door and around
the tailgate to the passenger side—*squirrels, mice, rats,
raccoons, woodchucks, moles, voles,
beavers, gophers, opossums*—
enumerating his catalog of services
the way contractors do their *retaining walls, patios,
porches, decks, roofs, siding, masonry*. This man
specializes in Rodentia. I found him
under Squirrels. I have squirrels under
my roof, squirrels in my walls, squirrels
in my sleep. "The largest rodent in the world
is the capybara," he whispers to me
as we stand together gazing up
at the suddenly conspicuous silence
emanating from my ceiling joists.
(They seem to know he's here.)
"It's a hamster the size of a sheep
or a sow. There's a family of them
at Southwick Zoo, across from the kangaroos,
catty-corner from the Patagonian
cavies. I visit them when I can." His plan
is to figure out where they got in,
set his humane traps, catch them one by one,
then plug the hole and drive a hundred miles west
to the Berkshires. "Any closer than that
and they'd find their way back." I like this guy
with his ladders and cages, his mercy and rodent
trivia: "*Rodens* is Latin for gnaw. They all
gnaw because they all have two incisors
that never stop growing. And gnawing
is the only way to keep them short. So you can't
blame them." I don't blame them. I thank him.
I pay him. And part of me wants to go with him,
ride shotgun out to the Berkshires,
keep listening, learning, rethinking
Rodentia, a large family of gray squirrels
barking and chirping in the cargo bed,
the names of rodents encircling us.

Flirting with the Deaf

I've been watching you watching the
interpreter. She is just to the left of the
speaker, and always slightly behind
so that you are always slightly behind
too, your face registering surprise
when the surprise has already been,
your smile on the heels of the other smiles,
your laugh coming after the wave of
laughter subsides. I love the lag time, the
pause between word and sign, the space
between signifier and signifier and
signifed. I want to slip inside that space and sit
across from you, legs crossed, hands
folded in my lap. If I made myself very
small, inconspicuous, insignificant as
another pair of antennae on the wall,
just watching you, quietly, watching the
interpreter, could I, could we, fit?

The Face of Listening

The active listening of Deaf people
in their signed conversations
with each other, if you've ever
seen them—beautiful, flitting,
leaping—communication as communion,
the almost-genuflecting heads
nodding their affirmations,
their agreements, their understandings,
the backchanneling, the feedback,
the empathic finger-flicked HOW-AWFUL,
the bobbing OH-I-SEE,
incredulous TRUE-BIZ?
in-the-face WOW! the approving
and allowing and concurring
RIGHT-RIGHT and YES-YES
and THAT-THAT-THAT—
all that grammar of the face, its tenses,
its *anima,* the thousand outpouring faces
of Deaf people listening to each other's
gab, palaver, repartee, the found
poems, the stories, jokes and autobiographies
in a language with its own music—
rhythms, assonances, crescendos
and descrescendos, riffs and repetitions—
all the sections of the body's orchestra—
hands, face, eyebrows, eye-gaze,
lips, tongue, head-tilt, shoulder-turn—
creating meaning simultaneously—voila—
a visual-gestural symphony for the eyes.

Sunday Morning

It was a mostly Jewish neighborhood
but up on Main Street there was a church
with a sign out front: *Jesus Saves.*
I had heard of Jesus and I was saving
for a new bicycle myself,
so I leaned my old bicycle against a tree
and climbed the front steps
and tried the front door. It was unlocked, unlike
the Essex Savings Bank across the street
where I had an account with $32 in it.
I stood there on the threshold, hesitating,
until I heard someone say, "You are welcome."
So I said, "Thank you,"
which was the first backwards thing
among a whole host
of backwards things I saw and heard
as I tiptoed in and took a seat in the last row,
which was the first row if everyone
turned around and faced the sunny
summer Sunday outside.
But they were all facing the darkness up front.
And when my eyes adjusted I saw angels
on the walls and ceiling,
and people standing and people kneeling,
and people waiting in line to go up front
where a man in a white robe deposited
something into their mouths.
Then they made these signs on their heads and chests
not unlike the third base coach in baseball,
and pretty soon someone was tapping my shoulder
because it was my turn now
to go up there for the deposit.
And that's when I ran outside and down the steps
and started pedaling as fast as I could
back into the sun.

Ergo Ego

It came to him in the shower. Which was where he got all his best ideas. He was thinking about himself. Actually, he was thinking about other people thinking good things about him. Which always made him feel good. Happy even. Ego is a source of happiness, he thought to himself as he rinsed the conditioner out of his hair and stood a little longer under the jetting streams, considering the possibilities. Then he smiled to himself as he stepped out of the shower, the same self he couldn't quite see in the fogged-up mirror, which he wiped clean with a corner of the towel, then padded over to the laptop in the kitchen, his wet footprints evaporating as he searched for Ego on the baby-names website. Nothing between Egbert and Egon. Hmm. But he couldn't help noticing that December, January, and February—sources of happiness for people who love winter—were popular, non-gendered names. "What would it take," he asked his wife, the bulging bowl of her belly obliquely reflecting the salad bowl in which she was tossing their lunch, "for Ego to make the cut? Think self-esteem, self-worth, self-love, ergo a source of happiness, the kind of happiness you'd want to name a child after." She stopped tossing, gave him a withering look. It withered the lettuce, the lunch, the whole family tree down to the little blossom curled up inside her. "It would take what linguists call a semantic change," she said, "which could take a few hundred years. But not in a million years would I name a child of mine Ego. What is the matter with you? Are you out of your tree?" "OK," he said. "Forget it. It was just a thought." A not entirely unworthy one, he said to himself.

Money

"I'm paying with cash," he says.
"Real money. Not plastic. Not
numbers in a cloud. Real smackers
that you can hold in your hand
and smell. Like in the old days.
I miss the old days." And he smacks
the crisp twenty in his hand,
sniffs it, lays it on the counter
and smooths it with both hands.

She waits three beats, picks it up
and puts it in the register, tap-tapping
a roll of quarters against the drawer,
the real money spilling out in a clinking
cascade. She counts out his change,
presses it in his palm. "Hell," she says,
"if you miss the old days, why not pay
with cowrie shells. Or better yet, a camel
or a cow. Livestock was the first money.
And it smelled like money."

Perfect Disappearances

This poem is for all the writers
writing. On their laptops, desktops, smartphones,
legal pads, napkins, palms
of their hands—desperate to get it down
before it disappears
like the phone number of the most amazing person you just met
and have to see again—just have to—
so you write it on your own skin
and walk off into the world alone
with the whole world in your hand. God
help the writers in love with the words that disappear
like disappearing trains you catch
by running after them,
losing a shoe, a hat, an earring, a spouse—a lifetime
of chasing the disappearing words,
breathlessly reaching for them,
grabbing hold and hoisting yourself up
onto the caboose, entering the rhythm
of those corridors moving through the world
as you move through them, feeling your way,
looking up and down and all around for
that dream you dreamed and followed all the way here.

Gift of the Acadians

He was the only Deaf person in his family. And he kept to himself mostly. Because no one in his family bothered to learn how to sign. He didn't learn it himself until they sent him away to the school for the Deaf, where he lived during the week. He only came home on the weekends. For years and years. And home began to feel less and less like home. Because the language of home wasn't his language. Because ASL was his language. So home was the school for the Deaf where everyone signed. And that's where he met his future Deaf wife. She took his last name, which was an old French name. A name that went all the way back to the French Acadians who fled Nova Scotia during *Le Grand Derangement* and settled in the American colonies. And the French Acadians kept to themselves mostly. Because the American colonists didn't speak French. So there was a lot of inbreeding—cousins marrying cousins—which must have been how a recessive genetic quirk got passed all the way down to the little Deaf boy. Who thought he was the only one. But he wasn't the only one. His wife was Deaf and pretty soon they had their first child, and that child was born Deaf. And he and his Deaf wife didn't know what to think. They laughed and rejoiced. And two years later, the twins were born Deaf. And they laughed and rejoiced again. And again. And home was ASL. And he and his Deaf wife and children were home. And he was never so happy in his life. A life in which he had thought he was the only one. But he wasn't the only one. Because the others were all on their way. And they'd been on their way all that time. They were a long time coming. But here they all were now. And he supported his growing Deaf family by working for the post office as a letter carrier. He delivered letters for over forty years. By the time he retired he was a grandfather. And his four grandchildren were Deaf. And their tiny flying hands and beautiful animated little faces were a gift. And this was the gift of the Acadians. This quirky, genetic gift. And it was a precious gift in spite of what the doctors and audiologists said. It was a hidden gift that took a long time to be found. But a short time to unwrap. The gift of a large Deaf family—Deaf children, Deaf grandchildren, Deaf sons- and daughters-in-law. All signing up a storm. All gathered around the old Deaf grandfather. Who was never so happy in his life.

Song

Sex is weird, don't you
think? I mean take my nose
in your handkerchief. I mean
who doesn't want to rub up against
Beauty? Get a little of it on your
eyelids, in your nose, get inside its
dark, sweet, monogrammed folds
for a good sneeze? It's a little
weird, a little gross, but I would
kiss you where you pee if you would
let me. Bless me, don't you think it's
Fate? I mean you and me in Beauty's
corner? I mean me rooting for Beauty
in your lap? And don't you think
Whoever thought this up was
Weird? I mean what was She
thinking? Love is life licking itself
prolific. I think it's all just one big
Tongue. And I don't think it means
anything. And I think about it all the
time. I mean all the time. Don't you?

The Rub

"You like?"
She barely
spoke English.

"I like."
I met her my junior
year abroad—

Gauloises.
Baguettes.
Croque Monsieurs.

Art museums.
"You like?"
"I like."

I stopped
going to class,
hung out with her instead,

smoking and drinking
Beaujolais and Stella
Artois. I learned

some French
that wasn't in the book.
She gave me

her tongue.
I gave her mine.
I knew her

intimately
and not at all.
And that was

the tragedy:
To like or not to like
was the only

question.

I Will Die in Florida

which is the state with the prettiest name,
according to Elizabeth Bishop
who died in Boston, Massachusetts,
according to Mark Anderson from West Virginia
who had read more Bishop than I had
when I met him at that college on the Hudson
where we were English majors. *Venereal soil,*
said Wallace Stevens about Florida,
or so said Robert Kelly, our professor and resident poet
who weighed over 400 pounds. I didn't care for Stevens
and I didn't care for Kelly and I stopped writing poetry
after graduating from that college on the Hudson,
though ten years later I started again and I haven't
stopped yet. Mark Anderson liked John Crowe Ransom
and Robert Penn Warren and Waylon Jennings.
Today he teaches English in a high school
in West Virginia. I liked e.e. cummings and May Swenson
and Paul Simon. Today I work as a sign language interpreter
in Boston, Massachusetts. We both liked Donald Justice
who lived and wrote and taught in Florida. I will die
in Florida, Mark Anderson will die in West Virginia,
Robert Kelly would have died a long time ago
if he hadn't lost the weight. Elizabeth Bishop
was an only child, like me, and published sparingly. John Ashbery
replaced Kelly as the resident poet at that college on the Hudson,
but that was a long time after I'd moved to Boston
and signed up for that first sign language class. Ashbery died
in New York at 90. I never cared for Ashbery
and I never cared for New York, though I grew up in New Jersey
just a stone's throw from the City. *A stone's throw*
in sign language is the thumb and forefinger
grazing the tip of the nose in a downward motion. I will die
in Florida because I married my sign language teacher
who was Deaf, and it didn't work out, so I married another
Deaf woman, which didn't work out either, so I married a third
Deaf woman and the third time's the charm—I never cared
for Florida but my third wife has convinced me
to retire in St. Augustine, where I'm sipping my tea
as I write this, a stone's throw from the Florida School for the Deaf
and the Blind. There are many live-oaks here in St. Augustine
uttering joyous leaves of dark green, the moss hanging down
from the branches, like in that Whitman poem

about a live-oak growing in Louisiana all alone. I will die alone
in Florida because we all die alone, perhaps remembering a poem
by Donald Justice, whose poems were short and memorable—
most of them fit on a single page—and whose output was small,
and who was an only child, like me, only in Miami.

Hotel Ars Poetica

The reader
is a guest here
and you're the manager
and the bellhop
and the maintenance man
and the boiler in the basement
needs a tune-up
and the doors that open clockwise
and the doors that open counterclockwise
need oiling
and everything needs polishing
and some things always need fixing
like the line breaks
even if they ain't
broke
period
and all punctuation
is optional because
we don't coddle our guests
we treat them with
you thought I was going to say
respect
didn't you
but the operative word is
intelligence
and another operative word is
and
and and and and
because this hotel has many rooms
and it employs
an additive syntax
and intelligence
and humor
and you're the night auditor
and the devastatingly handsome
pool boy
and the bellhop
and the maintenance man
so you better
start maintaining baby
and give the reader
a hand

The Idiot

This dusty old Dostoevsky novel—
one of the great books I never read
but lugged around with the other great
unread books as I moved from house to house

to this house finally, where I'll probably
die before I get around to reading this book,
old and moldering as it is, and I am. And I am
such an idiot, I think to myself, it's time
I threw out this book.

They called me Dostoevsky when I was a kid
because it kind of sounded like Hostovsky—
at least the tail end of it did—
and because I told them, "One day
I will be a famous writer, mark my words."
What an idiot!

I've been calling myself an idiot
a lot lately. Too much, probably. I'm not very
nice to me. If somebody else kept calling me an idiot,
I'd walk right up to him, my face in his face,
and ask him what his problem was—

What's your problem? I ask myself.
Yeah you. Yeah that word you keep calling me—
Do you want to make something out of it?

Dostoevsky was bellicose and testy.
He hired a stenographer, Anna Snitkina,
to help him write *The Idiot*
and *The Gambler.* He tested her dictation
by deliberately speaking so fast she couldn't keep up.

Then he married her. Then he gambled away
all their money. Then she took over
their finances and his publishing negotiations
and saved the day. He was a literary genius
and an idiot. She loved him anyway.
End of story.

"Life Is Sacred"

Yeah but
how do you know
it's so wonderful
not being dead yet?
I mean death is a wonder—
there's no getting around it—
everyone wonders
where the dead have gone.
There are theories of course.
Theories of God, theories of heaven.
And science claims to know,
but science has made a bigger mess
of the world than God did,
if God did make the world,
which science says He didn't.
Between you and me,
I think we're all asleep in heaven
dreaming the world.
Life is but a dream,
like it says in that song about rowing
a boat, the one we sang in kindergarten.
It was a round, remember?
Different people coming in
and going out at different times.
And it went on that way
for a long time until it all ended.
And then no one was singing.
Which felt a little sad but the silence
that hung in the air afterwards
was full of smiles.

Love Poem

I don't like the way you read
and I don't mean
aloud. I mean you read too fast,
too facilely, too faithlessly.
I mean we both read that book
and loved it—you said you loved it—
but then you moved on to another book,
another voice, while I still had the voice
of that book in my head
and I couldn't move on. I went back
and lingered in the copyright history,
the blurbs, the epigraph and dedication,
then I reread the first sentence, the first
paragraph, the first page,
and it was like love at first sight a second time
as I dove back into the book we loved,
and I'm loving it still
and reading it again. Don't talk to me
about the book you're reading now.
Don't tell me you're loving that book.
You don't know what love is.

Beauty

The way her hands danced across the braille page, it was a beautiful choreography to behold. Her left hand beginning each line, handing it off to her right hand halfway across the page, the right hand finishing the line as the left moved down to begin reading the next line. Left hand to right hand to left hand to right hand. Expert, fleet, like a concert pianist, or like relay runners in a race, the handoff accomplished seamlessly over and over, line by line down the page, page by page through the book, book by book through his entire childhood.

Was there ever a time when he didn't know it? He'd learned it with his ABCs, fingering the raised dots with his small hands, sitting in his mother's lap as she read to him aloud from the print/braille children's books while he looked at the pictures. B was *but,* C was *can,* D was *do.* M was *more.* M with a dot five in front was *mother.* White dots on a white page, but they cast these tiny shadows so he could see them in the light. Like a country of igloos as seen from an airplane on a sunny winter morning.

Having blind parents was as unremarkable as having breakfast in the kitchen, having mail in the mailbox, having rain on rainy days and sun in the summertime. Lending his mother or father his shoulder—his elbow as he grew taller—was like offering his arm to the sleeve of his own jacket, like giving his hand to his other hand. He thought nothing of it, didn't even have a word for it until he started kindergarten and the word got spat on the ground by some ugly mouths on the playground, older boys snickering and pointing, mimicking his parents as they swept their white canes back and forth, back and forth. *Click sweep, click sweep, click sweep.*

Those white canes. At home they leaned quietly against the wall like backslashes in the unpunctuated dark. Or else they sat folded underneath a chair or table like bundles of long chalk, a red one in each. K was *knowledge.* P was *people.* And the braille dictionary in seventy-two volumes was stacked practically to the ceiling, like a cord of wood.

His mother would stop reading, open her watch then close it, *click,* reach under her chair for her cane and open it, *chick-a-chick,* into a white line which she swept across an invisible line which she walked, out the door and down the street to the grocery store. Q was *quite,* U was *us.* Braille was dots in a cell, lots and lots of cells. Each cell was a three-story building at dusk, the lights on in certain windows, not others. Each book was a city, where he and his mother looked through the windows, their *fingers* pressed to the panes.

Outside it's beginning to snow. And each snowflake is a different character in the Complete Works of Beauty, which contains no mistakes that he has ever been able to find. And he has looked—he has spent a lifetime looking—but has never found a single mistake.

Thomas Lux, Poet Who Celebrated the Absurd, Dies at 70

—*New York Times obituary*

I don't think he would have appreciated that.
And I don't mean the dying, or even
the number—a nice round respectable number—
so much as the choice of the adjectival noun: *the absurd.*
Or is it a nominalized adjective? He would have
liked the question, the not quite knowing, or caring,
or saying one way or the other in the poem,
if it were his poem. Which I like to think it sort of is
now that he's dead and the writer of his obituary
got the headline wrong (like getting the headstone wrong)
and it's left to me to right it: Thomas Lux
celebrated *life* (which, OK, is, granted, sometimes, yes,
absurd). He celebrated *truth.* "I like the story because
it's true." And *beauty.* And *love.* Always love. Which is
"always, regardless, no exceptions... blessed." It's a missed
opportunity, he called it in his workshops, when we don't
call on the right words, the ones that are dying to be chosen,
as though sitting in a classroom with their hands raised
high, higher, practically levitating in their seats. *Absurd*
isn't the right word. He was funny, yes, but dead
serious about the poems. He had fine, caramel hair
as long as a girl's, but he had a mean lefty sidearm
that always hit home. He had lousy eye contact in front of the class,
or when standing up at the podium reading his poems,
but his gaze in the poems is laser, unflinching, lapidary.
Not a bad list, he would have said (three or more
adjectives make a list) but you can do better. Write
harder. This poetry business is hard work. "The thing
gets made, gets built, and you're the slave..."
He slaved over every word, every pause, every line break.
"You make the thing because you love the thing."
We love his poems because he loved them enough
to make us love them. *Absurd*? "Give me, please, a break!"

Stealing Home

It was a mostly Jewish neighborhood. Down at the schoolyard Billy Schachtel was at bat. Richard Cohen was on first. Jon Winkelried was on second. *Schachtel* means *box* in German. *Little box.* A pack of cigarettes is a *Zigarettenschachtel.* But none of us knew that. Because we didn't speak German. And we didn't smoke cigarettes. We were little. We were only in fourth or fifth grade. *Shtetl* means *little town* in Yiddish, a little town of Ashkenazi Jews in Eastern Europe before the Holocaust. But this was after the Holocaust, about twenty years after, at the bottom of the 9th in the schoolyard of South Mountain Elementary School in a mostly Jewish neighborhood in Millburn, New Jersey, in the United States of America, where Jews played baseball. Jews on shtetls in Eastern Europe didn't play baseball. And they never won. In fact, they usually got slaughtered. Schachtel swung and missed. We pronounced it Shack-TELL. Billy Shack-TELL. Not unlike William Tell, the folk hero of Swiss historiography. William Tell was a contemporary of Arnold von Winkelried, who threw himself on a Hapsburg spear in the Battle of Sempach, which created an opening for the Swiss Confederacy to rush in behind him and win the day. Winkelried was about to steal third. Cohen was on first, and maybe because the Cohanim were the Jewish priestly class, descendants of Aaron, brother of Moses, tribe of Levi, Cohen was able to judge that Winkelried was about to steal third. So he got ready to steal second. Which is called a *double steal* in baseball. With a judicious eye, Schachtel let the next pitch go by. Spoiler alert: Winkelried stole third, and he went on to steal home, and he went on to graduate from the University of Chicago, to get a job with Goldman Sachs, to work his way up until he eventually headed the Bonds Department and became richer than Croesus, the legendary king of Lydia, a kingdom in ancient Anatolia. Coney got thrown out at second, which was a kind of sacrifice that allowed Winkelried to steal home, not unlike the sacrifice that Winkelried's namesake made at the Battle of Sempach in 1386. It was the winning run at the bottom of the 9th, so Shachtel never finished his turn at bat. Because we'd already won, unlike the other Jews, the Jews of history, who almost always lost, and never really had a home.

Longevity

For as long as I live
I will keep coming back here,
making the trip alone
because there's nothing to do here
and no one to see here
and nowhere that isn't
not here. Standing across the street
from the house I grew up in,
which is the house I couldn't wait to leave,
I stare a long time at the nothingness
that no one else can see. Only I
can see it. I, the famous discoverer
of my only childhood.
I, the fastest kid on my block
until someone else was faster.
And then there was some question
about whether I was second fastest
or third. Somehow I slipped
into obscurity and adulthood
and no one has heard of me now
in my sixties, limping around
my old stomping grounds, my gimpy
leg smarting. I can't stop staring
at the old house—with its new
owners, new vinyl siding, new
roof with those expensive
metal shingles. There is no question
it will outlive me. I, who was famously
fleet-footed and immortal
back in my pimples.

Acknowledgments

The poems in *The Bad Guys* first appeared in the following magazines: *Bluestem*: "The Only Question"; *Coe Review*: "My Underpants"; *Comstock Review*: "Gauguin's Grandson"; *Earth's Daughters*: "The Emperor's New Clothes"; *Mud Season Review*: "Hitler Stamp"; *Off the Coast*: "Dooley for State Rep"; *Red Booth Review*: "Dueling Banjos," "Rebound Banjo"; *Sein und Werden*: "Bobby Bro"; *Spillway*: "Spiritual Mom"; *Switched-on Gutenberg*: "The Meteorologist's Breasts"; *Toasted Cheese Literary Journal*: "Works for Trumpet"; *Verse Daily*: "In the Home for Vehicular Manslaughterers by the Sea"; *Your Daily Poem*: "To the Lady Who Gave Out Pencils on Halloween."

The poems in *Is That What That Is* first appeared in the following magazines: *Blue Hour*: "My P.U."; *Clade Song*: "Cleaning Out the Rabbit Cage"; *Descant*: "Poem"; *Ibbetson Street*: "Nothing to Say," "Bar Mitzvah Boy Considers the Lobsters in the Tank"; *Kentucky Review*: "One Ambition"; *Mad Swirl*: "Visine"; *Off the Coast*: "The Calculus"; *Poets Online*: "Deaf and Dumb"; *Seems*: "Feckless," "The New Criticism"; *THAT Literary Review*: "Privilege"; *The Writer's Almanac*: "Erica," "Happiness"; *Your Daily Poem*: "Lion."

The poems in *Late for the Gratitude Meeting* first appeared in the following magazines: *Caesura*: "First Line"; *Connecticut River Review*: "Feel Better," "Practice"; *Galleywinter*: "Late for the Gratitude Meeting"; *Orchards Poetry Journal*: "Granted," "Wild"; *Poetry*: "Caterpillar"; *Poetry Virginia*: "Lesson"; *Poets Online*: "Dans Juive"; *Rise Up Review*: "Roll Over Bell"; *Slant*: "Bidet"; *South Florida Poetry Journal*: "Life Is a Banjo"; *Spank the Carp*: "Comma."

The poems in *Mostly* first appeared in the following magazines: *Aji*: "The Thing Is"; *Galleywinter*: "Trump Inaugural Poem"; *Glimpse*: "Going Back"; *Hawaii Pacific Review*: "Barbershop"; *Leaping Clear*: "Good Book"; *Literary Accents*: "Premature Ejaculation"; *Mad Swirl*: "Poem at the Breakfast Place"; *Necessary Fiction*: "Anonymity"; *Sein und Werden*: "To the One Who Stole a Book at My Poetry Reading"; *Solstice*: "Vernal Scrooge"; *Spillway*: "That She's Beautiful"; *Under a Warm Green Linden*: "Love Letter to Carl Sandburg"; *Upstreet*: "Talent"; *Vox Populi*: "Wording"; *Wordgathering*: "Authorized."

The poems in *Pitching for the Apostates* first appeared in the following magazines: *Abandoned Mine*: "Do"; *Beaver*: "Cocksure"; *Big Windows Review*: "Bess"; *Blueline*: "Fishing Vest"; *B O D Y*: "Bicycles"; *CCAR Journal*: "Pitching for the Apostates"; *Diode*: "Affiliation," "Forsythia"; *Freshwater Review*: "Jacob and Esau"; *Havik*: "Striptease at the Ars Poetica"; *Hidden Peak Press*: "Quits"; *Ilanot Review*: "Landmark," "The Story of the World"; *One Art*: "Interesting"; *Only Poems*: "Old Basketball Hoop"; *Poetry East*: "Homegoing," "Sleep by Howard"; *Scapegoat Review*: "Wilkinson Swords"; *SLAB*: "The Curiosity Factor"; *South Florida Poetry Journal*: "His Last Poem," "Nightmare"; *Star 82 Review*: "Prison Poetry Reading"; *TheIR*: "Best Listener"; *The Woven Tale*: "Commandment," "Throwing the Books Away"; *Untenured*: "Those Meetings"; *Young Ravens Literary Review*: "Letters from Camp."

The poems in *Perfect Disappearances* first appeared in the following magazines: *10 By 10*: "Over the River and Through the Woods," "Stealing Home," "Tassel of Wheat"; *Acumen*: "Passage"; *Bluebird Word*: "Beauty"; *B O D Y*: "Diminutive Wildernesses," "Frieda"; *Clade Song*: "Rethinking Rodentia"; *Compressed Journal of Creative Arts*: "Gift of the Acadians"; *Feign*: "Ergo Ego"; *MEARI*: "Window"; *Minyan*: "Golden Rule Revised"; *Naugatuck River Review*: "Sunday Morning"; *Off Course*: "The Rub," "Thomas Lux, Poet Who Celebrated the Absurd, Dies at 70"; *Only Poems*: "Flirting with the Deaf," "Song," "The Face of Listening"; *Please See Me*: "Life Is Sacred"; *Prairie Home*: "Money"; *Slant*: "The Heart Is Hard to Find"; *The Woven Tale*: "Emu"; *Thirteen Bridges Review*: "Perfect Disappearances."

About FutureCycle Press

FutureCycle Press is dedicated to publishing lasting English-language poetry in both print-on-demand and Kindle formats. Founded in 2007 by long-time independent editor/publishers and partners Diane Kistner and Robert S. King, the press was incorporated as a nonprofit in 2012. A number of our editors are distinguished poets and writers in their own right, and we have been actively involved in the small press movement going back to the early seventies.

Each year, we have awarded the FutureCycle Poetry Book Prize and honorarium for the best original full-length volume of poetry we published that year. Introduced in 2013, our Good Works projects benefit various charities. Our Selected Poems series highlights contemporary poets with a substantial body of work to their credit; with this series we strive to resurrect work that has had limited distribution and is now out of print.

We are dedicated to giving all of the authors we publish the care their work deserves, offering a catalog of the most diverse and distinguished work possible, and paying forward any earnings to fund more great books. All of our books are kept "alive" and available unless and until an author asks that their book be taken out of print.

We've learned a few things about independent publishing over the years. We've also evolved a unique and resilient publishing model that allows us to focus mainly on vetting and preserving for posterity poetry collections of exceptional quality without becoming overwhelmed with bookkeeping and mailing, fundraising activities, or taxing editorial and production "bubbles." To find out more, come see us at futurecycle.org.

www.ingramcontent.com/pod-product-compliance
Lightning Source LLC
Chambersburg PA
CBHW072143090426
42739CB00013B/3266